A NOTE FROM THE PUBLISHER

Welcome to StarTracker Publishing, where we believe in creating value for our readers. Our team of experts is committed to delivering high-quality books that cater to the needs of our audience. We understand that today's readers are looking for books that are not only informative but also engaging and entertaining. That's why we strive to provide books that are compelling, persuasive, catchy, thought-provoking, and highly influential.

Our latest book is a must-read for all members of Iota Phi Theta, Inc.. We firmly believe that this book has the potential to leave a lasting impact and impression on its readers. It is a story that needs to be told, and we are proud to bring it to the world at large. The book is packed with rich history and, inspiring stories that will help readers gain more insight into the Founding members of Iota Phi Theta, Inc..

We highly recommend this book and hope it will be a long-lasting reference for the organization.

David Greene & Melissa Van Oss
StarTracker Publishing

THE FOUNDING

THE FOUNDING
THE BIRTH OF IOTA PHI THETA INC.

AL MICHAEL

StarTracker Publishing LLC

Silver Spring, MD 20910
www.startrackerpublishing.com

The Founding
Copyright © 2023 by Al Michael

First Edition

Paperback ISBN: 979-8-88760-002-4
Hardcover ISBN: 979-8-88760-003-1

CONTENTS

INTRODUCTION

We often make pivotal life decisions that either enhance or haunt our lives. These decisions are often made about our careers, marriages, or personal relationships. Fifty-seven years ago, I decided to pledge to Iota Phi Theta Fraternity Inc., an unknown fraternity. If you ask why, I can only say that I was hanging out with my homeboys from New York City and Washington, DC and made the decision to pledge to the fraternity organization Iota Phi Theta, Inc.

What was the influence that motivated me to join this campus organization? I observed that members of this organization were older than me and more mature than me. They exhibited life qualities that I wanted to emulate. They were not your regular rowdy campus students; they were working in their respective communities and meeting the needs of the community. They were a unique group of Black men who exhibited the qualities of Brotherhood, Leadership, Scholarship, Fidelity and Citizenship: the Five Gold Stars of the Iota Phi Theta Fraternity Inc. These five stars are exhibited on the fraternity shield.

Let us take a look at the development of the organization during its formative years. Hopefully, this will clear up some of the questions often proposed by neophytes. This book attempts to answer many of the questions asked, such as, how did the fraternity begin? What was campus life like back then? What campus activities did the founders participate in? As a special feature, we will have guidance and direction from the Most Honorable Lonnie C. Spruill Jr. (1 A '63), the last living active Founder.

FOREWORD

In our fifty-nine years of existence, there are three books of our history in our library. Hopefully, this book will stimulate others to update both our history and our library. We are grateful for the opportunity to add onto our rich history with this book, and hope that others follow in the years to come. Hopefully in the future, given all the scholars we have among us, others will come forth and build on this book.

In the early part of October 2022, Founder Spruill called me and said, "Al, none of our history is documented. Somebody needs to write a book; our history is dying." Then he turned around and asked me, "Can you write a book?" I said, "Whoa!" I protested that idea. I said, "You know I was a math and science major. Incidentally, I failed English 101 and 102 in my freshman year, the only courses I received an unsatisfactory grade in, so I can't be writing any book." Founder Spruill convinced me to take a look at the idea.

Ironically, the company I work for has StarTracker Publishing Company under its umbrella. I returned to work and spoke with my partner, David Green, who studied at school with Founder Spruill, and of course he was encouraging. At this point both of them cheered me on.

Scholarship is one of our stars. Let this book be added to our library. I am seriously proud of the growth and development of Iota Phi Theta Fraternity, Inc., and it is one of my lifetime achievements.

FROM THE THIRTY-NINTH BROTHER TO PLEDGE IOTA PHI THETA FRATERNITY, INC. ALPHA CHAPTER 22 A '66

SPECIAL THANKS

I want to first thank God Almighty for giving me the wisdom and fortitude to create this book. Next is my son, Alfred Raymond Michael III, for without his IT support, development of this manuscript would have been slower. Also, thanks to my publishing team and coordinators, David Greene, owner, Alpha Bayou, IT Executive, and Melissa Van Oss. That also holds true for the people who made an earnest contribution to the success of this book.

DEDICATION

This book is dedicated to all Men of the Iota Phi Theta Fraternity,
Inc. "It takes a Man to make a Man."
With a special shout-out to:
Brother Harold David Ford, Jr. (5 A 1966), Sergeant at Arms
Brother Harold "Sonny" Jennifer III (17 A 1966) a.k.a. Lord North
Brother Dr, Richard B. Speaks (25 A 1966) a.k.a. Senior Suave
Brother Ronald Fassett (14 A 1966) a.k.a. Dinky
Brother Robert Redd (12 A '67) a.k.a. Boston Redds
Brother Kevin Bennett, Executive Director
Brother Anthony Workman, a.k.a. Capp

Founder Lonnie Spruill, Jr. Photo courtesy of Lonnie Spruill Jr.

WORDS FROM THE FOUNDER

My Brother, Al Michael, I am so proud of you for writing this book. There have been several others who wrote books about our beginning, but never one as comprehensive as this. I am Founder Lonnie C. Spruill Jr. (1A '63), the second Grand Polaris of Iota Phi Theta, Inc. and one of the twelve founders of Iota Phi Theta Fraternity, Inc. It took us a long time to be recognized by the Greek community. We were the last organization admitted to the Pan Hellenic Council. Prior to that, the last organization admitted was Sigma Gamma Rho Sorority in 1922. Our admittance changed the Council from the Elite Eight to the Divine Nine, and it took thirty-something years for us to achieve this status. My question is: where do we go from here?

Iota was founded September 19, 1963, on the steps of Hurt Gymnasium, Morgan State College. I am the last active living Founder that is breathing on this side of heaven, and I often ponder this question, again and again. We have increased in numbers and in maturity, and we have expanded in the community.

I am very proud of you, Al Michael. I was your Dean of Pledges. As for the book, it achieves my goal, which is to tell the truth about our history. On that note, God bless you, and God bless Iota Phi Theta Fraternity, Inc.

WORDS FROM THE GRAND POLARIS.
BROTHER DR. SEAN D. HOUSSEN SR.

Grand Polaris Brother Dr. Sean D. Houssen Sr. Photo courtesy of
Brother Dr. Sean D. Houssen Sr.

When I crossed over into this great Brotherhood in 1991 in the Beta Nu Chapter at Northern Illinois University, the idea of one day serving as the leader of this fraternity was not even a thought in my mind. Now, thirty years later, I have the distinct honor of serving as the twenty-third International Grand Polaris of Iota Phi Theta Fraternity, Inc. I am humbled, but ready; excited, but prepared. I am most thankful for the confidence in my leadership that you have shown me.

Under my administration, we will be One Iota—united in purpose, vision, and focus and working daily to live up to the lofty standards set by our Honorable Founders. "It takes a Man" is more than a motto; it speaks to the mature representation of fraternity life that is Iota. Brothers, we are built for this moment and times like these. Iota Phi Theta has a glorious past and an even more promising future. As the elected leader of this fraternity, it is my intent to "Be that Man" every day and serve the Brotherhood in a responsible and respectful manner.

When the community sees Charcoal Brown and Gilded Gold, they will know it represents a fraternity that embraces community service, civic engagement, leadership, and academic excellence. There will be no question as to the value we bring to our families, communities, and each other in fraternal brotherhood. This is not a part-time commitment on our part. Iota is a way of life.

Brothers, join me in building that tradition. Ow Ow

Yours in the fold,

Sean D Housen

Dr. Brother Sean D. Housen Sr.
Twenty-Third International Grand Polaris
Iota Phi Theta Fraternity, Inc.
Photo and document provided by Brother Dr. Sean D Housen Sr.

IN THE BEGINNING

Iota Phi Theta Fraternity was born during a turbulent era: the early 1960s.

The country was in flames. Racial disparity and discrimination showed its ugly face again. The African American community was disgusted and fed up. Slogans such as "Black is beautiful," "I am Black and proud," and "Burn Baby Burn" reinforced our commitment to change in this country. African Americans responded with protests, sit-ins, picketing, boycotts, and violence, which led to many arrests across the country.

One of these pockets of resistance lived across the street from Morgan State College at the newly opened Northwood Shopping Center, for Whites only. The shopping center housed The Hecht Company. You couldn't try on any clothes; all sales were final. At Woolworths, you couldn't sit down, and food had to be ordered to go. At the liquor store, you had to be at least thirty years old to purchase liquor. At Northwood Cinema, there were no evening sales to Black students. Most of the shopping centers were plagued by this disposition. The students, backed by some of the faculty, responded with racial discord through boycotting and picketing.

Founder Spruill stated, "We were over there every day, me and Founders-to-be Slade, Briscoe, Coakley, and Brown. Every time the police came, we would run because of our pending careers. No one could afford to be arrested." Some students made the sacrifice and were arrested. Most of the Founders knew each other previously through school affiliations, so there was no question of us getting together to combat this unjust cause. We did what we could.

Founder Spruill stated, "Our biggest challenge was getting onto Morgan State College campus. It was a headache, to put it lightly. We were portrayed as thugs, thieves, drunks, and womanizers, not to mention our street name, the 'I Felta Thigh Gang,' coined by Louis Hudnell." This campus attitude created many hinderances thwarting our progress. Most male Greek organizations were involved in blocking our progress.

The year before in 1962, Groove Phi Groove Fellowship, Inc. was founded on Morgan's campus, and now this organization, Iota Phi Theta Inc., another male organization diluting the potential pool of candidates. Let it be known that the only organizations that extended the olive branch of acceptance were Groove Phi Groove, Inc. and Phi Beta Sigma, Inc. As a matter of fact, that year Phi Beta Sigma, Inc. wrote an article in their annual journal about Founder Spruill and Iota Phi Theta, Inc., welcoming the organization to the campus.

For several weeks, we couldn't find a faculty member that would come forth and be responsible for us. Finally, Arthur Boone, a member of Kappa Alpha Psi, Inc., an audio-visual instructor, agreed to be our advisor, and the administration was satisfied.

Founder Spruill stated, "We repeatedly met with Dean Stanley, who was the Dean of Student Affairs, and he vehemently denied our access to the campus." Finally, after the sixth meeting, he consented to our request with sanctions and probation. For example, we had to have sweaters within the year. Allegedly, we had such a bad reputation, the administration had to have control over a bunch of non traditional students.

Several days later, on September 19, 1963, we ascended the steps of Hurt Gymnasium and declared our existence as family, friends and students observed our birth. That night, we all went to Maceo's bar in Northwest Baltimore (consequently my Line Brother Joseph Chapman bought this bar several years later, and we had several Frat meetings there), and Lenny Moore's bar put on a memorable celebration. By the way, Brothers, our middle name was "partying." We knew how to do it right.

Albert "Bus" Hicks was the first Polaris, with Charles Briscoe as vice-Polaris. Frank Coakley was treasurer and secretary because of his dependability, and Charlie Brown was Sergeant of Arms: a kickboxer needed to keep the peace among the Founders. Founder Spruill relates that several weeks after founding, Founder Albert Hicks was dethroned for promoting discord. Not only did he leave the organization, Albert left Morgan State college permanently. Founder Spruill stated that "the Polaris position was forced upon him by the Brotherhood" with Founder Lewis vehemently opposing his nomination. Founder Spruill stated, "He couldn't believe his partner in mischief was against him and the leadership of the organization." He believed it was jealousy. He couldn't believe the godfather of his firstborn would respond in the way that he did.

In our formative years, tensions existed within the organization. We didn't know how to disagree, creating tension that thwarted our progression. Founder Spruill stated that "when you have high strung individuals from the ghetto on a campus with the following characteristics of aggressiveness, combativeness, issues of moral turpitude, womanizing, theft of women, and a whole gamut of other personality dysfunctions, this is a cocktail destined to fail." I truly believed, as with my line, the Triflin 28, that some of the Founders had little faith in this idea, and within a year, three were gone, off to their prospective careers.

However, a couple of positive things began to happen. Mr. Thompson, manager of the student union, gave us a place to have our fraternity meetings on the second floor of the building. He firmly warned us that there wasn't going to be any fighting, drinking, drugging, or women at our meetings...members only. Our appointed meeting night was on Thursdays with six to eight Brothers showing up. Dues were fifty dollars a year, if we could collect it.

We also elected Miss Yvonne Howard as our Queen. She was fine—real royalty. What a lady. Everybody wanted to go with the Queen. However, First Line Brother, detective Jerry (Cullens 10 A '64) had that locked up. I first met her with my line at a party, and we weren't allowed to look at her after someone on my line commented, "Ooh wee." They kicked us out and sent us on our way.

According to Founder Spruill, "Things were looking up. Founders Coakley and I and Briscoe were invited to a campus meeting. It was campus election time 1964." Tyrone Baines, a member of Omega Psi Phi, had asked us to support his campaign for president of the student council in exchange for his support of us. We agreed, and they won, publicly acknowledging our support.

Our first year was productive, especially with the additional support of Alpha Kappa Alpha, Sorority, Inc., Delta Sigma Theta Sorority, Inc., Groove Phi Groove Fellowship, Inc., Phi Beta Sigma Fraternity Inc., add-on Alpha Phi Omega Fraternity, Inc., and last, but not least, Omega Psi Phi Fraternity, Inc. We were settling down and began to blend into campus life.

In 1962, Morgan State College had a mandatory four hundred-member mandatory ROTC program. Your Company Commander could have been a Kappa, Alpha, Sigma, or Que. My platoon leader on campus was a Pershing Rifleman. You had to work together on real-life military issues. Most of us were shipped off to Vietnam, if you didn't stay in school as long as possible. Something to think about. Some of us did not return.

My ROTC classmate Michael Brown was killed by a landmine after four weeks in Vietnam and another, Yancy Carrigan, came home with a partial plastic face. Some of us came back in pieces, not to mention the mental disorders the war created. In this mix, we paid attention to each other, and we blended in.

In the spring of 1964, we took on a line of fifteen. They were known as The Centaurs, and they were all local Brothers bonded by the local school system. Several were musicians: Willie Barber

'64), was a drummer; Harold Adams (8 A '64) a sax player; Rick Johnson (A '64), was a drummer; Calvin Freeland (13 A '64), military personnel; Ronald Wheatly (9 A '64), military personnel; James Watson (2 A '64), military personnel; Wesley Jennings (5 A '64), military personnel; and the Real Estate Guru of Baltimore, the brilliant and humble Daniel Henson (6 A '64).

Dan is my double Brother: I had the unmitigated gall to pledge Pershing Rifles Honor Society under him in 1965. I didn't find out until I got on the Iota line that he was in here also. Phew! Fortunately, at that time he worked a lot, and he didn't have enough time to give us his personal attention and best wishes.

A blessing came from that line in the name of Audrey Brooks, our Eternal Sweetheart. She was the mother of First Line Brother Wesley "Butch" Jennings (5 A '64). Mrs. Brooks was an administrator in Morgan State's administration office. Mrs. Brooks kept an eye on us, sometimes counseling us about our grades. Only a mother's love could have tolerated us, we were so often trifling.

From that line came Charles Briscoe's development of the current iconic shield and sweater. Founders did not have numbers on sweaters back then until the development of this line. Brother Wesley Jennings (4 A '64) was responsible for the development and assignment of numbers. I knew from our history that First Line Brother Jeff Johnson (5 A '64) had named this line The Centaurs. Brother Joe Hall updated us with the fact that the name came from the book *The Centaur* by John Updike, which Jeff felt characterized the disposition of the line.

Jeff Johnson. Photographer Unknown. Saved from a Facebook post.

Grand Historian
R.W. Richard V. Johnson

Polaris Richard V. Johnson. Photographer Unknown saved from an obituary pamphlet.

First Line, St. Line Brother Richard Johnson (1 A '64), made an effort to incorporate Iota Phi Theta by doing the paperwork (Article of Incorporation); however, these efforts fell to the wayside due to a lack of funds. However, he did draft our constitution and by-laws. Being a musician, he also wrote the words to our hymn from the tune of "Our Lady of Fatima."

In the fall of 1964, with the new line in hand, we entered the Mock Republican Convention on Morgan's campus, a big event of the time. Iota Phi Theta Fraternity, Inc. entered a team in that event. Members dressed in overalls and dawned pitchforks and rakes, which represented the plight of rural Black farmers in the state of Tennessee. To our amazement, out of the forty groups, we took second place, according to Founder Spruill. The fraternity was proud of this achievement; we could see our impact on the Morgan campus.

Participants that brought in that second-place trophy. Front row (from left to right): Lonnie Spruill, Harold Adams, Willie Barber, Lois Hudnell. Second row: Lawrence Brooks, Calvin Freeland and Frank Coakley. Photo courtesy of Dr. Willie Barber.

In the spring of 1965, a new line was initiated, and the line was comprised of three candidates: Alvin Pierce (1 A '65), Davidson Jones (2 A '65), and a third unknown Brother. For reasons unknown, Brother Jones dropped from this line; however, he came back the following year and pledged on the Triflin 28 line as (19 A '66). Brothers, our history was scant here, I imagine campus life was normal. I couldn't find any info for this period, so we might assume campus life was normal.

Founder Spruill stated, "In the fall of 1965, we established our first grad chapter in the basement of my house." The candidates were Brother Ernie "Kato" Donaldson, Sam Frier, Carme Pompey, and Bobby Wilson. Founder Charles Briscoe was the first Polaris of the first graduate chapter, Alpha Omega.

I knew two of these brothers. Ernie "Kato" Donaldson was the assistant dean of pledges of my line, the Triflin 28. Kato was small in stature and slim. He never raised his voice, was always a diplomat, drove a silver Chevy Corvette, and sold life insurance while putting himself through school. In the management of our line, he was supportive but firm.

On the other hand, there was the .45 caliber gun-toting Sam Frier. He was boisterous. At the football games, he was the head cheerleader of our section all the time. He packed his gun under his sweater, and once, I saw him pull it out at a game. Fortunately, no one ever got hurt. Brother Frier claimed he could carry a gun because he was a businessman. Brother Sam Frier would drive to New York City, purchase clothes, bring them back in his van, and tell everyone these were "hot" clothes. On any given day, he would pull up on Morgan's student union parking lot and sell clothes out of his van while classes were going on. I never saw him go to class.

Brother Pete Pompey was a 1970 Polaris and a renowned high school football coach. I never made contact with this Brother nor Brother Bobby Wilson.

Tragedy struck on December 4, 1965, when we lost our First Line Brother Lt. Anthony Watson to the Vietnam War. This was a crucial blow to many Iotas and the Morgan Community. Founder Spruill stated, "Tony Watson was my best friend. I met him in middle school." They enjoyed the same things: school, girls, sports, and family. Founder Spruill stated, "I went with his sister Muffy for two years. I was part of their family."

Founder Spruill further stated, "Tony did not want to go into the military because of the war. Unfortunately, he was drafted." Brother Watson reluctantly attended officer training school at Fort Devin, completed the same, and shipped off to Vietnam. In his letters, he let us know that he hated the place and longed to be home. His platoon was surrounded in a firefight, and all members were killed. When Brother Watson's body was returned to the United States, Brother Lt. Ronald Wheatley (9 A '64), went up to Dover Air Force base and accepted Brother Watson's body. Founder Spruill stated, "Brother Watson's service was held at St. Edward's Catholic Church down on Poplar Grove Street, and it was a service for a hero."

2nd LT James Anthony Watson's memorial flyer. Photographer Unknown. Taken from Facebook

In the fall of 1965, I took a calculus course with Brother Richard Johnson (1 A '64). Immediately, he was bending my ear about this new organization, Iota Phi Theta. I didn't want to hear anything about pledging. The previous semester, I had pledged to the National Honor Society of Pershing Rifles for fourteen weeks. They were the scourge and beast of the campus. I thought that it would enhance my military career. Rick couldn't tell me much about the organization, but he was always talking about it. Rick was also a drummer. A couple of times, my classmates and I would drive over to see him play in the Washington, DC area. For the rest of the semester, he promoted the organization to the members of the class. He couldn't sell me because I didn't see many members.

According to Founder Spruill, "The active founders were Brothers Slade, Coakley, Briscoe, Dorsey, Lewis, and Hudnell. We participated in all campus activities, shows, dances, football, and baseball games." Founder Spruill noted early Iotas were never invited to step shows. The campus knew we didn't have a team, so they ignored us. Founder Spruill had a dream: he was determined to develop a team before he graduated. Unbeknownst to him, the Triflin 28 was on the way.

In the spring of 1966, Morgan's campus was buzzing with smokers and interest meetings. "Come and take a look at us," was the theme. A pool of new sophomores were available. The campus was littered with salesmen and saleswomen soliciting for their respective organizations. There even was a slogan directed to the nonPan Hell organizations, and it was "Try Phi," which meant pledge Iota Phi, Groove Phi, or Alpha Phi as an alternative organization. By the way, Brother Johnson was now in my advanced calculus class, and he was at it again, relentlessly.

He invited me to the first interest meeting at the student union. I didn't go; although at the time, I didn't know he was familiar with two of my homeboys, Harold Ford (5 A '66) and Harold Sonny Jennifer (17 A '66). One day after class, these three ganged up on me about pledging. I finally agreed, promising to leave if it got out of hand.

The following Saturday, there was an interest line meeting at the student union. There were numerous candidates in attendance. Founder Spruill was the speaker. Looking around, I recognized him. We were all in ROTC together along with Brothers Ronald Wheatley and Calvin Freeland. This was a historical lie that swooned the whole audience. He stated, "We've got chalets, yachts, cars, and women in here." I believed him because on that day, in the student union parking lot, there were Corvettes, Rivieras, Tornados, and Cadillacs. I was impressed because I was walking at the time. Tough on dating, I must say!

The Iotas that week also had a smoker in which forty-four were in attendance, and finally, twenty-nine were accepted. I didn't go because I was preapproved. Some participants declined, and others were blackballed. Back in the day, if you didn't meet the frat standard, any organization member could blackball you, no questions asked. A blackball was powerful: it culled the known slackers, troublemakers, and cartoon characters out. Today, with civil liberties in place, an organization would lose its shirt if it denied any applicant entrance, so people drift into your organization to see if they want to belong. There are no challenges to pledging today as opposed to yesteryear; somebody's feelings might get hurt. Most Brothers that I have known have come in and enhanced the growth of our organization. Others have just drifted away, never to return, and that's a common phenomenon everywhere.

Finally, one night the line convened at the Druid Hill Park reservoir. Where else could you take twenty-nine pledges and not be noticed? The Founders had a logistics problem: there were so many of us and few of them. We had to drive all of the time, everywhere. No surprises there. As we jogged around the reservoir, we were told to count the spikes in the fence that protected the reservoir. We came up with some numbers like 1,253 spikes in the fence—that's what we told them collectively. The Founders liked the answer because it showed unity.

As with the Founders, there was tension on the Triflin 28 line. Triflin 28 had several subgroups despite being a unified line outwardly. The Baltimore Brothers were jealous and contrary to outsiders. The Brothers from New York and Washington, DC were told to go someplace else. We were just too slick for them. Myself and Harold Ford (5 A '66) were going to fight the line president, Robert Young (1 A '66), and big mouth James "Sluggy" Jackson (16 A '66), brother of Reggie Jackson, the baseball player. Founder Spruill called a meeting and threatened to disband the line if we didn't desist. It was making us look bad. We still kept them at arm's length, working with them on a few community projects such as car washes, clothing drives, and waistline parties. (For those of you who don't know about waistline parties, your waist determined your price of admission to an event.) We were active in the community, doing small things.

Session nights were always on a Thursday night. One night Founder Spruill and Big Brother Donaldson took Howard Stanback (26 A '66), Thelps Evans (13 A '66), and some others to Leakin Park. Founder Spruill and Brother Donaldson were roughhousing with the pledges, and all of a sudden, Howard Stanback picked up Founder Spruill above his head and threw him down an embankment. Founder Spruill sustained a burst knee, which required stitches at Sinai Hospital, and his silver silk suit was torn in the knee. Also, my Line Brothers stole Lonnie and Kato's keys and hid their Chevy Corvettes. The next day, Founder Spruill, being the leader that he was, swept everything under the rug and kept everything on the down-low. He was satisfied: they had guts.

The Iotas partied often, and they had a lot of women at their parties. Many of them were not students. I used to call them "in-town girls" because they had nothing to do with the campus. They could stay out all night and party as long as they wanted to.

It was at one of these parties that I was introduced to the Queen of Iota Phi Theta. Her name was Miss Yvonne Howard, and she was pretty. We individually introduced ourselves to her, but just as we started to get comfortable, the heavy voice of Brother Jerry Cullens (10 A '64) said to us, "Don't look at her no more." Soon, we were on our way out the door, for that was a party for the Big Brothers. That Friday night, we were on our way to our next project. I did get the inference that the Big Brothers were proud of us, developing a line of our magnitude and prowess, which was reflective of them was quite an achievement.

Halfway through the pledge period, Founder Spruill and others felt that we should commemorate the memory of Anthony Watkins, whom we had just lost to the Vietnam War several months earlier. We decided to go back out to our old haunt at Druid Hill Park reservoir and have a mock burial ceremony. My Line Brother Jimmy Penn (23 A '66) was to portray Tony Watson, and he was going to be buried in the park at midnight. With picks and shovels, the line hustled out to the park and started to dig a shallow grave. A line of that magnitude drew attention anywhere we would go. Lo and behold, three police cars showed up to address the disturbance. We all thought we were going to be locked up; that night, however, we had Detective Jerry Cullens (10 A '64) of the Baltimore City Homicide Division with us. He intervened and called the police officers off. We had to desist in digging the grave and leave the park. They told us to get out of the park and take the ceremony somewhere else.

Around the fourth week of pledging, Founder Spruill wanted us to create a routine for an up-and-coming campus step show after several suggestions and demonstrations because we had talent.

Robert "Half" Young (1 A '66), President of Line came up with "The Centaur Walk," best described as a two-step walk from side to side, which reminded me of the musical group The Temptations. Well, when we snaked that line into that Auditorium, with twenty-eight of us doing that walk, the crowd went crazy. The screaming and the hollering was deafening. They had never seen anything like that before. Note well, my Brothers, Iotas never stepped before the Triflin 28. We were never invited and didn't have a team to compete with.

Around the fifth week of pledging, we lost a Line Brother because of his employment. Aubrey "Skip" Wyatt (29 A '66) had to quit or lose his job. He was my roommate, and he stayed down in the dormitory for the pledge period. Skip, Line Brothers Ronald "Dinky" Fasset (14 A '66), and Dwight Stith (4 A '66) all worked down at the Jessup Cut: that was the Maryland Penitentiary in Jessup, Maryland. They were jail guards. Dinky and Dwight worked out with their times with their supervisors, but there was no agreement on Skip. Unfortunately, he could not participate in Hell Week, so we were down to just twenty-eight people. Many of us have always deemed him as "The Eternal Centaur": the first Brother that did not complete the pledge process. The following year, he went to law school in California. End of story.

Hell week was upon us, and we were still running the reservoir at night counting the spokes in the picket fence that protected the reservoir. This brought a couple of extra Big Brothers out; they just questioned us as to who we were. Hell week was a breeze. We did a number of car washes, yard cleanings, and menial jobs that gave us exposure.

One night, they had us on Gwynn Falls Parkway and the Western Maryland train trestle. We were standing in the gas station next to the trestle wiping cars down at midnight. Brother Briscoe had us practice saying good night to him. It was all in fun. He was driving a new Ford GT Mustang 351cc: white bottom, black top, with four on the floor. Remember, at this time, I'm still catching rides, so I would notice something like that. Founder Briscoe left the parking lot in a cloud of dust, wheels spinning, positraction rear end dancing. He drove down the parkway, made a U-turn, then made another, and came back down the parkway toward us at a high rate of speed.

When he passed us, he crashed the car into the bridge trestle. We were all in shock; we all ran to the car. I could see he had a big contusion at the dead-center of his forehead where his head hit the windshield. There were no seat belts back in the day.

His first words to us were "Don't let no blood get on my sweater, or I will *******!" Carefully, the Brothers wrapped his head in a towel and removed the sweater. Another Line Brother gave him his shirt because the Founder had to go to hospital on that one. Before the police came, we rolled the car up into the gas station with the front end facing the gas station. I saw Founder Briscoe a day later, and he acted like nothing happened. My conclusion was that this guy is as tough as nails. Thank God. It could have been worse.

Hell Week was upon us, anxiety was high, and we spent a lot of time getting prepared. We knew it could be any night because other lines started going over. Finally, word came down to meet in front of the student union at 9 p.m. Founder Spruill and Brother Donaldson met us in the parking lot, and after putting on our masks, we entered the building. We were led into a poorly lit room, and there were Founders and First Line Brothers in the room. We were ordered to sing the line songs we created, and then there was silence. We were ordered to unmask, and in the center of the room was the shield all aglow.

On April 19, 1966, the 11:00 p.m. ceremony began, and by midnight, we were Iotas. As they say, we galloped into Iota land. We were taught the handshake and allowed for the first time to sing the hymn. We knew the words to the hymn but were never allowed to sing it. Also, we were given our certificates and twenty-eight sweaters. The sight was overwhelming. That night, there was much handshaking and patting each other on the back. We finally made it.

The next day on Morgan's campus, Founders, First Line Brothers, and neophytes plastered the campus with brown, white, and gold sweaters everywhere; a beautiful sight. We had just enlarged our footprint on Morgan's campus, blending in further and getting stronger and stronger.

As historic as this event was, no one remembers anyone taking photos of this line. We were not a camera-carrying culture at that time.

Since there was only one month of school left, most of us had to prepare for finals. During the month, we did attend our first Alpha Chapter meeting election.

Yearbook 1966. Photograph courtesy of Soper Library, Morgan State University.

Robert "Half" Young (1 A '66) was the newly elected Polaris for the coming year. There was talk about establishing another line, planning of money-making events for the coming year, and talk of expansion. It was suggested that the out-of-state Brothers spread the word in their home states. I made contact over the summer while in New York with later-to-be Brother Robert Bounds from Norfolk State, whom I played summer league basketball with. Many promising ideas were developed at that meeting. I was impressed, and I developed a sense of achievement.

The fall of 1967 was non incidental. In other words, "all was well." We had our own sections at the football and basketball games.

We appeared at Murphy Auditorium for any performance events. We were there. We threw some good ass parties, a concoction of the Brothers, the women, and the wine provided a damn good time, always.

The fall 0f 1967 was non incidental. We participated in campus activities when available, and we would show for all football games and basketball games, the biggie being homecoming. We would throw a party at the Green Door, a basement club in the hood, and thirty to fifty people would come through.

At this time, in the fall of 1967 some brothers were promoting the frat, looking for potential brothers for the upcoming year. In the first week of March 1967, in the administration of Polaris Robert Young (1 A '66), a smoker, was held at the study hall, and twenty candidates were selected to pledge the spring line.

In an interview with Chuck Brown, '67 from Delaware, I asked him, "Why did you pledge?" Chuck stated, "One day I came home from class and my main homeboys all had ties on, and I asked, 'Where y'all going?'" Several Brothers informed Chuck that they were going to the Iota Phi Theta smoker on campus. Chuck said, "My boys Bernard, Ruffin, Earl, Gooby, and Hayes were going to see what it was all about, and I didn't want to be left behind, just in case." By the end, we all had submitted applications and were accepted.

Chuck stated, "Several nights later was the introduction of all the new lines on campus in front of Holmes Hall. We were allowed to do the Centaur Walk, which many people hadn't seen before. When we left the Holmes Hall area, the crowd followed us across the bridge, leaving the rest of the organizations to perform without an audience in attendance." Brother Bernard Hamm, stated, "We looked like The Pied Pipers," and the name stuck. That's how they got their name.

I can say that I influenced two Brothers onto the spring 1967 line of "The Pied Pipers." One was my roommate George "Peahead" Nock from Philly, who left our dorm room when he got on line because it wasn't safe for him to be my roommate. And the other was Robert Redd (12 A '67) a.k.a. Boston Redds, who later became my roommate in an inner-city house after he went over. This was a dynamic line of twenty brothers that had various talents, and for the first time, most were from out of state.

This line had multiple talents: they were football players, track and field participants, crooners, composers, choreographers, scholars, lovers, and later, some became Polaris. The songs, "Not Now (I'll Tell You Later)," "Valerie," and many others were composed by this line. The wood first came out with this line; many of the Triflin 28 were in high school fraternities, so the trend followed them to college. My involvement was limited due to my employment. However, if I caught you, you had to recite the Founders names, I would make you do pushups and then dismiss you upon signing your book, which was a first on Morgan's campus. Before, Iotas did not have enough brothers on campus to collect signatures.

Boston Redds (12 A '67) said, "I was livid that the Big Brothers took us out to Klan country during hell week and left them in a precarious situation. At midnight, people were staring and probably calling the police. We definitely didn't belong there." Fortunately, someone realized where we were, and we—all twenty of us—caught the last bus back to Baltimore.

Again, I wasn't involved much with the line because of employment, but a hilarious incident occurred involving four-foot-ten John "Stinky" Lanier (1 A '67). Lanier was "smelling his piss" and experiencing "little man syndrome." He wasn't showing respect, had a swagger, and was always talking out the side of his mouth to Big Brothers. As a result, we had to put him in check.

We—Harold Ford (5 A '66) and Harold "Lord North" Jennifer (17 A '66) a.k.a. Sonny—fixed all that. We drew a gallon of water and tried to make him drink it all. Of course, he didn't, but he drank three quarters. Since he didn't drink it all, we threw him into the cold showers down at the dormitory. It created a slight change in that he was humbled for the moment. Lesson: Ya don't mess with your Big Brothers. You haven't made it yet.

The administration did an excellent job in the development of this line. We all noticed the quality of these brothers on this line and developed them to their potential. Every week, they performed somewhere. So, after six weeks the Pied Pipers galloped into Iota land to take their place in Iota history. The date was April 20, 1967.

Yearbook 1967. Photograph courtesy Soper Library Morgan State University

The next day we overwhelmed Morgan's campus with those brown and gold sweaters, and the reactions from the campus community were congratulatory. A job well done by all brought this line to its potential because many leaders came from within it that directed the organization in the right direction.

Of course, for the four final weeks in school, we had the reality check of being immersed in preparing for finals, and we had to get back to the books to make sure we stayed in school. We did have our first chapter meeting with the Pipers, I just don't remember where. I know we discussed objectives from the coming year with the emphasis on expansion, fundraising, and another line. Out of state

Brothers were encouraged to promote Iota Phi Theta Fraternity over the summer in their home states.

In 1967, in order to meet the conditions as stipulated by Morgan State University; we had to create a plan of expansion. Yet the school still had its doubts about us. We moved forward meeting the conditions of expansion as proposed by the school. The first was to be Delaware State College sixty miles away. The rumor was that the connection was with Brother Chuck Brown. He has dispelled this rumor several times, pointing to members of the track team as the source of the connection.

Chuck Brown stated, "There was a team that went up to Delaware State four weeks in a row to prep these new centaurs." The team was Robert "Inky" Hawkins, Chuck Brown, Ruffin Bell, Eddie Hayes, Bernard Hamm, Ike Jackson, and some others. They interviewed them, put them on line, pledged them, and took them over. I remember driving up in a caravan of Iotas on the interstate, all of us going to see new Iotas go over. Brothers, that was a memorable occasion.

The making of the Hampton Institute, Beta Chapter was the bomb. The connection was Robert "Inky" Hawkins: his dad, a Kappa, was Dean of the College. Inky, being an outlaw, was not pledging his dad's fraternity, Kappa Alpha Psi, and instead opted to bring Iota Phi Theta onto Hampton's Campus. I am sure that all the Virginia Brothers groomed that line into shape. I made two trips to Hampton to meet these new Brothers. The first was to see what they knew, and the second was to see them go over. The Brothers of Beta Chapter went over what I believe on homecoming weekend. The campus was plastered with people, and we were in our sweaters celebrating: a real party atmosphere. The Brothers of Iota Phi Theta rented eight rooms at the Holiday Inn Scope and threw a going over party. It seems like the whole campus came because many of the girls violated curfew to attend this bash. Women and free-flowing wine—one of many good times back in the day. That night, a police officer came to the hotel and asked us to disperse at about 2:00 a.m., and we complied.

In 1968, two more chapters were made: Norfolk State and Jersey City. The connection for Norfolk State was our track members and Robert Boyd of Norfolk State. I had schooled Robert Bounds over the summer while in New York, and he did pledge on the Norfolk State line, but I never got a chance to shake this Brother's hand in Brotherhood. Mickey Barbee was the connection between Morgan State University and the new chapter Epsilon chapter, according to Brother Craig Brown. I missed all those trips because of a work schedule and trying to get out of school and stay out of the war.

EPILOGUE

Well, Brothers, this is it for me. As I said, this book was to cover the development of our formative years on Morgan's campus. I wrote about what I had experienced in the development of the fraternity. Information about this organization leaves here every day. A good example was the recent loss of Brother Wesley Jenning: at Founder Spruill's last birthday party, I jokingly told Brother Jennings that I was going to interview him last because he lived so far from the city. Because of this procrastinating, the Brother slipped out of here taking a wealth of information with him.

I didn't want any conjecture or sensationalism; the focus is the truth. I avoided writing about the negative things that happen to us, which if revealed, would demean Iota Phi Theta Fraternity, Inc. For those that know, let us take those negative incidents with us to our graves.

I hope that this book stimulates others to continue to document all of our important accomplishments, focusing on the truth. I cannot stress the importance of the loss of information, it does an injustice to us all. African histories were handed down by word of mouth; we cannot do that. If the truth gets distorted, it has no value. Future administrations should make this one of its objectives: preserve the truth.

In the Name of Iota Phi Theta Fraternity, Inc. OW OW (22 A '66)

PILLARS OF IOTA

Through the past half century there has been a consistent line of Brothers that continually gave of themselves, their families and has made major contributions to the Fraternity. Below are several individuals that have met that mark above and beyond. They have shared their bios and experiences in the development of the organization. Some family members have made comments also highlighting the careers and lives of deceased Founders. It is their generous contributions that give us the documented facts that enhance this book. The facts and statements provided are verbatim and permission has been granted to publish them by their respective authors. Perhaps, Brothers of the future could emulate some of these Leadership behaviors and continue to further develop the organization.

THETA MAN THURSDAY

IOTA PHI THETA® FRATERNITY, INC.

www.iotaphitheta.org @IPT1963

Photo and article provided by Kevin Briscoe

CHARLES "BANG BANG" BRISCOE

2 A '63
Secretary
1st Polaris Grad Chapter
Sons Narrative

My father, Charles B. Briscoe, Jr., was a founding member of Iota Phi Theta. For him, Iota was an all-consuming passion. From taking a hand in establishing the fraternity's rituals and traditions to personally designing its coat of arms, he played a vital role in building the organization from a one-chapter non-Greek local entity in 1963 into one that is now a full-member of the National Pan-Hellenic Council and includes more than 30,000 members in 300 chapters in the United States, the Bahamas, Columbia, South Korea and Japan.

Serving as Iota's third Grand Polaris while in school, "Bang Bang," as he was affectionately known, was the consummate Iota, and his influence on the upward trajectory of the gold and brown bond should always be remembered and appreciated.

There was a time that I didn't fully appreciate Bang Bang's work to build Iota.

I recall being at my grandmother's house on N. Monroe St. for dinner one evening with Dad, my Aunt Pat and my sister, Sherry. Full of myself as a newly minted member of Kappa Alpha Psi, I laughed at his suggestion that I should've pledged Iota.

"Did you even think about Iota?" he asked. "We've got almost 20,000 members."

Aside from considering the sheer hysteria that could have come from being a Briscoe pledging Iota in 1980, much less a founder's son, I dismissively said," Y'all ain't even Greek. Besides, we got 80,000 members!"

To his credit, Dad showed no remorse or offense to my playful insult. He simply replied, "You wait."

Over the years, I've certainly waited and watched as the tentacles of Iota Phi Theta began to envelope college campuses and young men of honor from all points on the compass.

When I was a small child, Bang Bang and the other founders deemed an Iota "mascot." With the title came a miniature Iota paddle that Dad made just for me. I later presented that paddle to the fraternity when it opened its national headquarters on N. Calvert St. back in the 90s. In my remarks at the ceremony, I remarked upon how Iota Phi Theta had grown from a small group of "nontraditional" students born from a decade of activism to a family of men dedicated to philanthropy and the well-being of all peoples.

In 2013, I was invited to Iota's 50th anniversary celebration in Baltimore. While there, I reveled in all of the fond—and often humorous—stories told by my founding "uncles" and stood in awe as present-day members spoke of Dad in reverential tones. At the conclusion of the event, I was presented with a pencil-drawn rendering of Dad framed in a gilded gold plate that brought me to tears.

At the time, I remembered that conversation from my Mama Libby's dinner table. When Dad said, "you wait," I had no idea back then that over the horizon of 60 years stood this magnificent D9 organization. If Bang Bang was still with me, I'd simply say, for me as your son and for countless Iota men, "Thank you; it was worth the wait."

I knew Charles Briscoe before he was an Iota, he was a frequent visitor to the neighborhood because he dated the girl next door for several years. Often, he would come through the neighborhood bragging about his sports prowess and play big brother to the younger fellas in the neighborhood. He would hit the ball so far down in the woods, you couldn't find it, he would often throw bullets at us, the ball was too hot to handle. Several years later, one evening brother Briscoe came up the street with this beautiful brown white and gold sweater on. I said, "Charlie what gang is this," he said, "this is a college fraternity sweater." It was the first time that I ever saw the sweater. That had to be the spring of 1964. Second time I observed the sweater was when Founder Briscoe and other founders entered an automobile on Morgan's campus. Then I knew he was telling the truth, I was impressed, never knowing what the future held for me. My opinion of Founder Briscoe was that he was a great man. He exhibited all the attributes of the stars, "Leadership, Citizenship, Fidelity, Brotherhood, and Scholarship."

In the fall of 1968, he commandeered a horse and a flatbed wagon to create a homecoming float. With many female students, volunteers and Brothers they created a brown and gold paper-mache float with the shield. He didn't put the Queen on the float, Yvonne Howard, this genius put Moms on the float. Moms was an 80-year-old canteen attendant, who was popular and fed many students under the table, back in the day. That was an automatic win. We got the 1st place trophy. What a win! The after celebration was up at Maceos Bar that night…Another no parking available situation.

Photo and statement provided by Dr. Marcia Coakley, Franks Wife

FRANK "SPANKY" COAKLEY

3 A' 63

1st Treasure

In a recent interview with Dr. Marcia Coakley, Frank's wife, I asked her what your most fondest or precious memories of Frank were, she replied, "I have two occasions which were my favorite. The first was dating Frank for the first time. Dating back then had its challenges. Frank was a blind date referral from a friend. My son used to screen out prospective gentlemen. One day Frank came to my house and my son basically interviewed him before he could see me, he came into the room and said Mom he's okay. I don't know what Frank said to him, but he was impressed with Frank. Frank took me to a banquet and what I noticed was that we were sitting down front, in the VIP section when I opened the program for the event, I noticed next to Frank's name was the word founder. I was astonished because he never said anything to me about this. This was the humbleness of Frank, most guys would have bragged about something like that, but not Frank."

I asked what was the second most memorable occasion with Frank. Mrs. Coakley stated, "that they had been dating for several years and she wanted this situation to change; she didn't want to be a date for the rest of her life. At this point she recommended to Frank that they separate and they did. They didn't see each other for several months but kept in phone contact." Founder Spruill added," that during this period Frank was very moody, didn't socialize and was somewhat withdrawn."

One day Frank called and said, "what time can I pick you up for church tomorrow?" She knew that this question was out of character, because Frank would have asked first, if she was available. They made a decision to go to Frank's Church, this was a pivotal point in their relationship. Not seeing Frank for several months, she realized at that point the separation had taken its toll on Frank. Frank lost a considerable amount of weight and he was very reserved. Mrs. Coakley stated, "you just don't know how the decisions you make affect another person." Subsequently, they were married soon thereafter.

I asked Founder Spruill what his most favorite memory of Frank was. Founder Spruill stated, "I knew Spanky since we were 3 years old. I ran away from home when I was 7 years old because my father would not buy me a decoder ring for 25 cents, so I could get the secret messages from the Captain Video Television program, so I packed my clothes and went to Frank's house several blocks away. His mom welcomed me with open arms. When I went upstairs to speak to Frank and told him what the story was, Frank offered me an extra decoder ring that he had. Boy was I relieved, several days later while we were in school Frank told me that I owed him 25 cents for the decoder ring. I thought he gave the ring to me,. words went back and forth and I finally paid him over a period of time, but I thought he gave me the ring. so it was a trick on me."

Founder Coakley was the founder that I had the most contact with. One day, I had just come out of a meeting in which I lost my job. The new director of the company, Universal Counseling decided we weren't going to council children anymore. We were going after the drug and alcohol clients which I wasn't licensed for. Upon learning this information of course I was distraught, I left the office building wandering the streets of downtown Baltimore, and who should I run into but Founder Coakley immediately when I saw him I blurted out what had just happened to me. Not asking him how he was and after I finished telling him what just happened to me he told me I just lost my job as vice president at Maryland National Bank. Boy, did I feel bad he couldn't convince me to let's go and have a drink somewhere. I just had to be by myself. I will never forget how supportive he was despite the fact that he had the same problem.

For approximately 15 years Frank's company would always sponsor a VIP table at the Morgan State University Gala. He always made sure that I had two free tickets for myself and my guests to attend the Gala every year. Frank was one of the hosts of the St Mary's Jazz Brunch. I used to always buy at least a half table and bring friends or Brothers. I want to thank Frank for all the games, meetings and events that we attended. It was always a pleasure to see him. His attributes were his diplomacy, his logic and his empathy for others, a gentleman's gentleman.

One day, Founder Coakley and myself attended a friends and family day at the church of Brother Brian Murray, we were the only two Iotas there at the time. I knew that he was somewhat reserved, he didn't have the signature smile that he was noted for. He wanted to tell me something and finally he told me, and he had asked me to pray for him because he just recently found out that he had cancer which was a shock to me. I thought he was invincible but these things do happen, so we prayed and I guaranteed him my support.

After the onslaught of the virus, contact was very limited, I never knew his status, six months prior to his death my mom passed.

Photo taken by Art Lawson

Last contact I had with Founder Coakley was at Founder Slade's funeral.

The article penned below is by Clarence "Tiger" Davis, to be found in the National Association of Black Veterans Inc. 2023 issue.

President of 2nd Groove Phi Groove Inc line 1964.

Early Comrade of Iota Phi Theta Inc., Frank Coakley and the Founders

Sunrise - October 1, 1942

Most Honorable Founder

FRANK B. COAKLEY

In the mid-1960s, Stokely Carmichael uttered the term, "Black Power" which became synonymous with the violence of that era although it had absolutely nothing to do with the anger which poured into the streets of America. Nevertheless, "Burn Baby, Burn" was attributed to the public concept of Black Power.

Black power was the unification of African People to pursue political and economic Power. This required capital which was not readily available. As they say, "those in power" will never extend that opportunity to those lacking power. As the suppression and violent responses became more prevalent, the religious community and business leaders realized that change had to come.

Vehicles were established and personnel was recruited to manage banking within the inner city. Knowledgeable and committed professionals maneuvered the maze of institutional racism to provide the necessary capital to the African American economy. One of the proponents of the movement for economic opportunity was Frank Coakley.

Frank, a U.S. Army Veteran, appeared to be quiet and unassuming yet he was one of the most prolific builders of the black economy in Maryland. Frank never saw himself as a distinguished leader of the Black Power movement, though his footprint and spirit cannot be separated from the achievement of economic parity in Maryland.

A pioneering banker with Maryland National Bank, Coakley was recruited by Mayor Kurt Schmoke (1989) to establish a lending program to assist Baltimore neighborhoods. In 1995, Governor Parris Glendenning appointed Coakley to be Assistant Secretary, of the Maryland Department of Housing and Community Development and the Director of Community Development. He was Chairman of the Board for the Morgan State University Foundation and a member of the Board of the Fire and Police Retirement System.

He raised thousands for scholarship funds and other charities including his church. He was a founding member of Iota Phi Theta Fraternity in 1963. Daniel Henson, the former Baltimore Commissioner of Housing, viewed Coakley as "the definition of a gentleman's gentleman." Coakley was inducted into the Baltimore City College Hall of Fame. Today, NABVETS Baltimore Chapter is proud to assign Emeritus Status and render him immortality.

Photo and article provided by Daniel Henson

MY IOTA LIFE-1964-2023
DANIEL P HENSON, III

I should have been the 13th Founder!!

I was on Morgan's campus all morning on September 19, 1963 and ate lunch in the Canteen with Lonnie Spruill, Frank Coakley, Webster Lewis and Bus Hicks. But, I had a job and left campus around 2:00, and recalled waving to Charlie Briscoe and Lou Hudnell as I headed to the bus stop. When I got to school the next day, all the guys were talking about was "I felt a thigh," some new club/fraternity they had decided to start as opposed to pledging one of the existing groups on Morgan's campus.

The group of guys were all town dwellers, i.e. not living in dorms on campus, not a part of campus life. Usually gone after 5:00. Most were the first of their families to attend college, as was I. No particular traditions to uphold. Some of them were older than other college students and several were married and/or veterans. They/we knew each other generally from parties and high school activities prior to coming to Morgan.

But, I was not the only one who missed being "on the steps on the 19th." There were others who had been long time friends of some of the "Founders" and who felt they should be #13 too. And so, the decision was made that we would form a pledge line. I thought that we should be included automatically since the only difference between us and them was that we were not hanging out on the steps of Hurt Gymnasium that afternoon watching the girls go by on that particular day, but Lou Hudnell insisted that we pledge and his loud voice carried the day. By the time we started, there were 15 of us and we were subjected to random hazing, but all went over. Like several of my other brothers, I had previously pledged the Pershing Rifles, which was physically and mentally challenging. But, it was based on the tradition of a national organization. Pledging Iota, with no traditions, was PR + 1.5. Contrary to popular belief, we did not have line numbers or names for the line or nicknames. Years later, the late Brother Wesley "Butch" Jennings did his best to fit our line into the proper protocol. I became 6A64.

Unintentionally, we established several traditions, mainly based around Morgan's Homecoming, ourselves. Charlie Briscoe was a master of invention. He created several paddles and a shield, giving us the basis for future designs. It was 1964, and Briscoe had a Ford Mustang convertible. The theme for Homecoming that year was "The Wild West." We created a hitching post and other decorations in front of Holmes Hall and tied the Mustang to it with a rope after we rode in it during the parade. We won the contest for creativity. John Slade was on his way to becoming a media star and he admired John F. Kennedy very much. He even was able to imitate JFK's Boston accent and affected many of his mannerisms. John entered an on campus presidential debate and won on behalf of Iota.

1964 was a big year in my life. Not only did I become an Iota for life, but I married my high school girlfriend, Del. My blood brothers (I have 4) and my Iota brothers made up the wedding party. A few months later, Del and I moved into our first apartment in West Baltimore. It became the de facto frat house where we hung out and partied. After graduation in 1966, I taught school in Baltimore for a year and then got a job selling life insurance in 1967. In 1969, I was promoted to sales manager and was able to hire almost all Iota staff. At various times, Lonnie Spruill, Gary Burgess, Tex Dean and Frank Clay were part of our award winning team.

While I played very little part in on campus activities after I graduated, I stayed in touch and took on legal and political challenges for Iota. Iota began establishing grad chapters in about 1970 with the formation of Alpha Omega.

I helped to draft and file the Articles of Incorporation for Iota, Inc. I helped to draft Mr. Arthur Boone as our on campus advisor. Later, in 1993, I was working for Baltimore City which had recently foreclosed on a building in MidTown at 1600 N Calvert Street, and I helped to acquire it for "Iota." Today, that iconic building serves as Iota's international headquarters. I served on the board of the National Iota Foundation for a few years and helped to get it incorporated.

Today, I am a proud member of Gamma Omicron Omega (GOO) Alumni Chapter, a Life Member of Iota Phi Theta Fraternity, Inc. and a recipient of the Thomas "Tex" Dean Distinguished Service Award. I still take it very seriously that we are "Building a Tradition, not Resting on One."

DR. WILLIE BARBER

7 A '64

Photo and article provided by Dr. Willie Barber
Name: Dr. Willie L. Barber
Where born: East Baltimore, Maryland
Parents: Jay S. Barber & Rosa L. Barber
Siblings: Jay S. Barber, Jr, Shirley Barber, Juanita Barber, W. George Barber, Kevin Barber and Karenthia A. Barber.
Education: Attended Dunbar Junior and Senior High School Graduated with a Bachelor's Degree in Music Education from Morgan State University, and a Master's and Doctor's Degree from Howard University.
Years at Morgan: 1961 to 1966
School Activities: Marching and Symphonic Band, ROTC
Life Hobbies: Music, swimming
Girl Friends: I am not telling
Wives: Shirley Patricia Barber (married to my high school sweetheart for 56 Years).
Children: Noel M. Barber and Myles D. Barber
Grand Children: Amyhr Barber, Noah Barber, Jayde Barber and Nazaiah Barber
Employment: US Army, Social Worker Patuxent Institution, Social Work Supervisor Rosewood Center, Foster Care Supervisor Baltimore City Department of Social Services, Assistant Director Talbot County Department of Social Services, Program Director Maryland Department of Human Resources, Social Work Professor Bowie State University, Chair Social Work Department Bowie State

University, Social Work Professor Morgan State University, Group
Facilitator Center for Urban Father's and Families, Human Services
Consultant and psychotherapist for Thrive Behavioral Health LLC.
Musician for various bands including my own.

Awards: Outstanding Musical Services to the Baltimore City
College Choir, Member of the Year for the Maryland Regional
Practitioner Network for Fathers and Families 2000, Author for
"Strong Fathers, Strong Children, Strong Families and Strong
Communities A Guide for Responsible Fatherhood"

Certificate of Completion of all levels of the Knights of the 21st
Century Curriculum

Certificate of Appreciation in recognition and appreciation of
Dedicated and Continued Service to the University Community
Social Work Club Bowie State University

U. S. Senator Benjamin Cardin Certificate of Special Recognition
at the Annual Music Diversity and Scholarship Awards Banquet

Certificate of Appreciation from Barbara A. Mikulski United
States Senator, to Dr. Willie Barber (Teacher, Community Servant,
Author, Percussionist and over 30 year veteran of Music) for out-
standing dedication and commitment to the Music Industry

Maryland House of Delegation Official Citation for being a music musician, author and graduate of Morgan State University and
Howard University (Delegate Ruth M. Kirk).

Baltimore County Executive (James T. Smith, Jr. County
Executive) for being named a 2010 Rosa Pryor Music Scholarship
Fund Honoree for my dedication to music that has enhanced count-
less lives throughout the community.

The City Council of Baltimore Resolution in recognition of
my passion and dedication for music, my enthusiasm for all things
academic and my contribution to music education (City Council
President Bernard Jack Young

Congressional Achievement Award for my commitment to the advancement of music in our community. (Elijah E. Cummins, Member of Congress)

The Department of African American Studies University of Maryland Baltimore County in recognition of my artistic contributions to the tradition and development of Jazz music (Chari, Dean, Arts & Sciences and Chancellor)

Recognition of Christian Services and Devotion from the Deacon Board of St. Paul Baptist Church Rev. CC Alexander, Armstead C. Jones, Chairman

Executive Producer of three CDs ("Responsible Fatherhood with Willie Barber and Friends," "Old Time Religion plus Praise and Worship Equals Gospel Jazz with Willie Barber and Friends" and "Celebrating the Birth of Jesus with Willie Barber and Friends"

Photo provided by Dr. Willie Barber. Photographer Unknown.
Brothers Harold Adams and Willie Barber along with Founder Webster Lewis and non Brother Rucks

This picture was taken at The Casino, in Baltimore, on Pennsylvania Avenue on any given night. I followed these Brothers religiously from The North End Lounge, The Bird, Cage, The Haven Lounge, The Closet Bar, Peyton Place Bar, any place where good music could be heard. It was always a pleasure hanging out with them.

THE ATLANTIC COAST REGION OF IOTA SWEETHEARTS, INC

IN LOVING
Memory

MAY 23,1921   DECEMBER 27,2003

Eternal Sweetheart
MS.AUDREY S. BROOKS.
Forever grateful for your presence and graciousness

Photo Ms. Audrey S. Brooks. Photo courtesy of Iota Sweethearts Group on Facebook.

I didn't know Audrey Brooks during our formative years at Morgan. I knew she was an administrator at the registrar office, but I never really had not made any contact with Mrs. Brooks. It wasn't until toward the end of her life that we made contact. You know that women talk, as fate would have it, Mrs. Brooks met my mother at a gospel soiree, sponsored by my mother's senior citizen building Stadium Place. As women will talk, one word led to another, and both of them identified that they had sons that were members of Iota Phi Theta Fraternity Incorporated. Mrs. Brooks asked my mother to have me call her. Subsequently, she asked me to come over to her house. After hugs were exchanged she said to me, "Al Michael, former Grand Polaris Jerry Pittman takes me to my doctor's appointments when needed. And I want you to get my medication every month" and I replied, "yes ma'am." I attempted to get her to get her medication every 3 months but she said, "I can't count all those pills," I said, "yes ma'am." Case closed.

Maybe three times a year, I would take them for a ride out to Loch Raven Dam or transport them to an event which was rare. You had to have the following conditions, everyone feeling good, good weather and good attitude. They would chatter in the back of my car about everything, nobody wanted to sit in the front. If we were out long enough somebody would take a nap…humorous. I did take my mother to one of her final birthday parties at the Forum Caterers which was attended by many. Soon thereafter, she passed away. God bless her and thank her for her guidance.

Brothers note well: The article below is the best researched article that I have seen, about Iota Phi Theta Fraternity, Inc. It contains comprehensive data about the development of the organization and numerous other tidbits. That is a must know. I send special thanks to my Line Brother Arkley "Pete" Johnson, 18 A '66 for its development and permitting me to use it. Job well done, Brother.

Photo and excellent article provided by Arkley Johnson, 18 A'66
Triflin 28

THE HISTORY OF THE IOTA PHI THETA FRATERNITY, INC.:

FROM CLIQUE, TO CLUB, TO FRATERNITY, TO NATIONAL ORGANIZATION

Compiled/Edited by:
Arkley (Pete) Johnson
18A66
First Edition: October, 1974
Revised: September, 1976

Prologue –

When man became aware of the difficulties of complete isolation, he found various means of survival within groups. The process of banding together is a very natural phenomenon, whether the purpose is survival, economics or social intercourse. There appears to be an even stronger likelihood for individuals of similar interests and beliefs to gravitate toward each other: this is the impetus of most fraternal groups, and so it was with the founding members of the Iota Phi Theta. However, we cannot take this to embody the complete essence of brotherhood.

We shall see that a true sense of fraternity was not to be realized until a good deal later on. What did exist initially was a special group of men. Men who were older than the average college student: men who worked full-time jobs, men who had families and other responsibilities; and men who had neither time nor inclination to play children's games. Time, this far has proven the latter consideration to be the most significant underlying factor in the philosophy of Iota Phi Theta brotherhood.

What is it that makes one man feel so close to another that he comes to regard this person as his brother? What is the bond: common interest? age? color of skin? Mutual beliefs? Admiration? Personal need? It may be all of these or none of them. There is an intangible element without which the others are null and void. Simply stated, the element is awareness: the awareness that every man has the right to be his own person, without compromise, no matter how subtle the individual differences may be. This is—the pivotal point of the force which binds us together. Elements of similarity serve to bring people together and what remains is the means by which individuals discern their own uniqueness.

This being the case, what need is there for subjecting one's fellows, one's future brethren to physical abuse in the name of discipline? This certainly does not preclude the need for a sound body, but if initiation is little more than an endurance test, we can hardly consider ourselves responsible proponents of the Iota philosophy of brotherhood.

Each man, though one among many men, is still very much himself: with or without Iota. The concepts of a fraternity, especially a black fraternity, cannot be reconciled without considerations of this creed. The struggle must continue and black organizations must recognize the roles they play in unifying and teaching.

The founding brothers, though not entirely free of pretense, had a keen sense of purpose and timing. To date, the tenets set down by them have established the basis upon which Iota has grown and survived and will continue to grow. This document will present the factual account of the beginning and early existence of Iota Phi Theta. Due attention will be paid to our weaknesses and shortcomings as well as our strengths and triumphs.

Beginnings

Social interests are among the many unifying factors which promote group development, and such was the case of Iota in the embryonic stages. On the 19th of September, 1963, twelve men, all long time acquaintances, stood on the steps of Hurt Gymnasium, on the campus of Morgan State College. They discussed the formation of a campus social club which would serve their needs without the constraints imposed by the initiation rituals characteristic of other organizations. They were originally dubbed I FELTA THIGH by Louis Hudnell. It was soon realized that, since the group would function as a campus organization, some alterations would have to be made to ensure a serious reception by the campus community. Thus, the metamorphosis entered yet another stage: from clique to club to fraternity. The name was appropriately changed from I FELTA THIGH to the similar sounding IOTA PHI THETA by Lonnie Spruill. This was to be a "Greek" fraternity in name only, but unforeseen events would force changes in the future. The twelve founding brothers of Iota Phi Theta are:

Albert Hicks – Polaris

Lonnie Spruill, Jr. – Vice Polaris

Charles Briscoe – Secretary

Frank Coakley – Treasurer

John Slade – Business Manager

`Baron Willis – Chaplain

Webster Lewis -- Historian

Charles Brown – Sergeant-at-Arms

Louis Hudnell – Dean of Pledges

Charles Gregory

Elias Dorsey, Jr.

Michael Williams

This stage was a time of innovation and creativity, for the symbolism we know today originated from the founders and first of our pledge lines. We now move to a description of Iota's unique symbols;

created not to conform to everybody else's, but to represent a new and vibrant organization.

The Colors: Brown and Gold

Charcoal brown and gilded gold were selected as the official fraternity colors to symbolize black (Negro at the time) brotherhood and the pursuit of monetary, scholastic and social enrichment, respectively.

The Star: Polaris and the Number 5

The head or president of an Iota chapter is given the title of Polaris which applies on local, graduate and national levels. This represents leadership and guidance, for just as Polaris (The North Star) guided ships and sailors through the night, the Polaris of Iota is charged with the leadership and direction of the fraternity. The symbol of the Polaris is a five-pointed star, each point having its own significance.

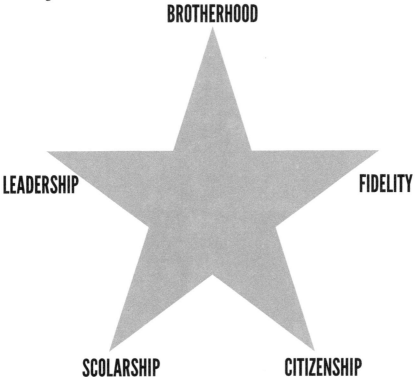

BROTHERHOOD

LEADERSHIP

FIDELITY

SCOLARSHIP

CITIZENSHIP

The numerical symbolism is also evident in the five stars which adorn the fraternity shield:

Central Star ... Brotherhood

Near Left Star ... Leadership

Far Left Star ... Scholarship

Far Right Star ... Citizenship

Near Right Star ... Fidelity

The Fraternity Shield:

The shield is an original design by Charles Briscoe, the founding secretary. Experts consider it heraldically incorrect, but the intention was to create something unique and dynamic rather than accept existing standards. The shield appears in two different versions: the one which is on all fraternity sweaters displays only the stars and the Greek letters IΦθ; the other version bears the Centaur, the flaming candle and the black cross with the twelve golden rays. These items are now discussed in turn.

The Centaur:

The life's blood of every organization is embodied in the quality of its new membership. The Centaur was chosen as the symbol of Iota pledge lines owing to the attributes of the mythological beast: the speed and stamina of the stallion in addition to the mental prowess of man. Centaurs, however, were wild, insatiable, rapacious creatures who, as such, necessitated either subjugation or destruction. Rather than subjugate or destroy, Iota attempts to mold the Centaurs into dedicated and responsible brothers while preserving their individualities. The Centaur was added to the shield in 1965.

The Candle:

A red candle with its dripping wax symbolizes the rough and winding path which the Centaur must follow to attain the light of Polaris embodied in the flame. The candle, used in all ceremonial and induction functions, was also placed upon the shield in 1965.

The Black Cross:

On December 4, 1965, Brother James Anthony Watson lost his life serving his country in Vietnam. As he exemplified the image of Iota brotherhood, a black cross with twelve golden rays was placed on the shield in commemoration in 1965. The rays emanating from the cross represent the 12 founding brothers.

At this junction, we continue with the chronological discussion of early history. Taking up the events shortly after Iota was founded; note that the major portion of the fraternity's development took place at Morgan State College, for, until late 1967, Alpha Chapter was the only existing undergraduate organization.

Iota has always been about the business of change; in fact, three weeks after the organization was founded there was a transition in leadership. Albert Hicks had to leave the school and Lonnie Spruill was made acting Polaris. The brothers began to function with the emphasis placed upon the mature image and all the related artifacts of the "mature man on campus." This was helpful as well as hindering the initial growth period: helpful in the sense that mature, level-headed individuals are essential to any organization. Hindering? If age is the only criterion for maturity then growth must be stunted on a campus where the average age of potential members was 3 to 5 years younger. On the other hand the artifacts of maturity: cars, clothes and women, tended to have a magnetic appeal for younger prospects. This does not insure quality membership in all instances, but it does build an attractive image. As a result there was a kind of polarization between the founders and the campus community at large. The brothers carried on many activities in Baltimore City due largely to the fact that they were not officially recognized on campus.

Despite these constraints, in March of 1964, Iota Phi Theta revealed its first pledge line of fifteen (15) Centaurs. The members of the first line were:

Richard Johnson	Ronald Wheatley
Frederick Howard	Jerome Cullens
Ronald Flamer	Lawrence Brooks
Wesley Jennings	Howard Williams
Jeff Johnson	Calvin Freeland
Daniel Henson	Charles Watts
Willie Barber	James Watson
Harold Adams	

They became brothers during the last week of April, 1964. The most significant aspect of the fraternity creed was demonstrated in the administration of this line. Pledges were initiated without excessive physical abuse and harassment; the initiation procedure was utilized more as a rite of passage rather than an opportunity to belittle or dehumanize. Iota Phi Theta feels that this is the only way to make good brethren. "It only takes a few weeks to pledge Iota, but it takes a lifetime to be a brother."

Around this time, Brother Richard Johnson made two very significant contributions. He wrote the original drafts of the constitution and by-laws which were later used as the basis for establishing Iota Phi Theta as a fraternity incorporated in the State of Maryland. Rick Johnson is also the composer/arranger of the fraternity hymn which was adapted from the song, Our Lady of Fatima in August of 1964.

During the course of the first line, the fraternity became active on campus and began to seek recognition by the administration and other campus groups.

The Drive for Acceptance—

In order to be a legally functioning campus organization at Morgan, a fraternity or sorority had to be affiliated with some governing body. In this case, that body was the Pan Hellenic council which was expressly for "'Greek" organizations. Although we were never fully accepted as peers, Iota Phi Theta became a trial member of the council, and in effect, obtained official recognition on May 13, 1964. The trial membership was based upon the contingency that a Beta Chapter be established in the near future. To be sure, our presence on the council was tolerated, at best, by the other groups. Iota received little, if any, assistance from our so-called peers; however, we were fortunate to have two valuable allies. Our faculty advisor, Mr. Arthur Boone, provided guidance and political influence during the early stages. Mrs. Audrey Brooks has always been in support of the fraternity and her position in the school administration helped to keep us from being victimized by our enemies.

During the homecoming festivities of September, 1964, we claimed first prize for the best float. It was during this time that we chose to honor those ladies who had aided and supported us. Miss Yvonne Howard was the first, official fraternity queen and Mrs. Brooks became the eternal sweetheart of the Iota Phi Theta.

On January 14, 1965, Iota's constitution was accepted by the administration of the college. Through most of this period the chapter's officers were:

Charles Briscoe ... Polaris
Fred Howard ... Vice-Polaris
Rick Johnson ... Secretary
Baron Willis ... Treasurer

Although things were looking great at the start of 1965, there were events to come which would deal crippling blows to the fraternity.

The Dark Days —

Functioning under the jurisdiction of the Pan Hellenic Council soon proved to be a serious handicap. We were forced to adhere to their membership criteria which were restrictive and preempted growth. This became painfully clear when we had our next line: only three individuals were eligible for membership, and consequently, only one brother was made in 1965: Brother Al Pierce. The administration of the Alpha Chapter at this point consisted of:

Lonnie Spruill ... Polaris
Danny Henson ... Vice-Polaris
Calvin Freeland ... Secretary
Lawrence Brooks ... Treasurer
Louis Hudnell .... Business Manager

At the end of 1965, tragedy struck with the death of James Anthony Watson on December 4th. Lieutenant Tony Watson was killed leading a night patrol in Vietnam. This event accompanied a period of low morale for the fraternity. Spruill and Hudnell left school which created a void in the fraternity's management.

Rick Johnson became Polaris with the Vice-Polaris slot left vacant. Other brothers left school at this time via graduation or dropping out.

The most positive by-product of 1965 was the formation of a fledgling group of graduate brothers. At this time, members were allowed to "pledge" into the graduate chapter. The officers and initial members of Iota's first graduate group, started in March of 1965, were:

Charles Briscoe ... Polaris
Jeff Johnson ... Vice-Polaris
Harold Adams ... Secretary/Treasurer
Ernie Donaldson
William Watson
Carmie Pompey
Samuel Frier

Through the efforts and dedication of the brothers, both in and out of school, iota survived 1965. Hudnell and Spruill returned and in February of 1966, Iota Phi Theta voluntarily left the Pan Hellenic Council and began to exist on Morgan's campus as an "outlaw" fraternity.

The Comeback —

To bear the brunt of scorn and ridicule as outlaws is not an easy task, but the pride and determination of the remaining brothers was more than equal to the job. At this time fraternity policy stated that every brother would have and wear a sweater… and they did. Attempts to repress them were rendered futile and subsequently, Iota held a smoker to attract potential members. The result was a line of 28 Centaurs which was later dubbed "The Trifling 28." To be sure this was not a model line: many were not serious at first; most of the pledges lived in Baltimore; and, like the founders, many were working and attending school part-time. On the plus side, this line had more than its share of popularity, and, though their pledging was taken lightly by other organizations, their vitality and appeal gained favor within the campus community. On April 19, 1966, the "Trifling 28" galloped into Iota land and began paying their dues. Friendships grew, songs were written and people began to respond. Robert Young (Half) the President of the line developed the famous Centaur walk which has become a fraternity institution. The effect of dozens of brothers performing with the Centaur walk is fantastic.

Another important outgrowth of the line of '66 was many contacts among campus-based students. It was this interaction and participation in campus life that enabled the next line, in 1967, to be composed almost entirely of out-of-state campus students. These twenty men, known as the Pied Pipers, were the most popular and talented group to pledge Iota yet. They possessed a drive and spirit which revitalized the older brothers and charmed the campus. This was unmistakably a turning point: not only has the gap between city and campus been bridged, but the way had been cleared which would allow the founding of new chapters. The "Pied Pipers" crossed the sands on April 30, 1967 and the era of the road trip en masse began.

The fraternity really began to expand in 1967 with interest groups organized at Hampton Institute and Delaware State College. The Hampton interest group was the first, founded by Robert (Spot) Hawkins. However, Delaware State became the first chapter established outside of Baltimore. Since there was no functioning national body at this time, both chapters had their founding members inducted by the Polaris of Alpha Chapter who was Arkley (Pete) Johnson at this time.

The expansion continued in 1968 with chapters being formed at Norfolk State College and Jersey City State College under John W. House, Polaris of Alpha Chapter. This growth period was gratifying, but the lack of a central authority would prove to be disastrous. In any event, the tide and high spirit moved forward and in November of 1968, Iota Phi Theta was officially and legally incorporated as a National fraternity with its base in the State of Maryland.

This concludes the account of the early history of Iota Phi Theta. This next section deals with the near-fatal problems of uncontrolled expansion, the resultant near-death of the fraternity and the emergence of a strong national body. This period, as you will see, was the most critical in our brief history.

IOTA PHI THETA -- 1969 to 1973

The rapid expansion of the fraternity toward the end of the sixties was initially envisioned as a positive process. However, this growth in the absence of a functional national governing body tended to weaken the organization. Something would have to be done to pull all the chapters and fractions together.

In the spring of 1969, under the leadership of John House, Polaris of Alpha Chapter, an attempt was made to hold a national conclave for the purpose of establishing a centralized organizational structure. This action precipitated the sudden appearance of incumbent national officers, who, although previously inactive, declared the conclave illegal and cancelled it. The results of this intervention destroyed momentum, lowered morale, caused resentment on the part of the Alpha Chapter and added to the general confusion regarding the future.

The situation was exacerbated later in 1969 when a chapter founded at North Carolina A & T insisted that they had not received a refund of an overpayment to the National Office. This caused controversy over fraternity finances and rumors proliferated which fostered resentment for the national office and a loss of respect for the organization as a whole.

The hiatus continued until the spring of 1970 when the Grand Polaris, Rick Johnson, resigned and was replaced by Carmie (Pete) Pompey who was then serving as Grand Executive Secretary. Pompey was a very dedicated brother who worked hard in an effort to undo the damage done by previous negative attitudes. Owing to his earlier lack of contact with the organization, favorable rapport with the brothers was difficult to establish. He succeeded in conducting the first national conclave in December of 1970 where an enthusiastic attendance discussed rules and regulations and awarded the first Tony Watson award to Alpha Chapter. Unfortunately, there was no adequate follow-up to this meeting and the fraternity continued to decline.

The fall of 1971, culminating almost an entire year of inactivity, found interest waning and morale almost completely crushed. Rumors proclaiming the death of Iota Phi Theta were widespread; organization collapsed, chapters were using different induction procedures and singing different songs for the fraternity hymn: uniformity was nonexistent. Alpha Chapter was still regarded as the national headquarters and resentment of the Grand Council had proven extremely intense. Stories of the creation of "phantom" chapters circulated. Failure seemed almost certain. The worst part of this situation was that most of the brothers seemed to accept it without making any effort to keep Iota alive.

The fraternity cried out for a unifying force, a capable leader who still believed in Iota. We needed a person who was familiar with all the factions within the frat and who could restore confidence and trust in the Grand Council. This task would require a tremendous personal commitment and, doubtless, a tremendous personal sacrifice. The national "elections" in November of 1971, saw Brother Thomas (Tex) Dean rise to accept the challenge. He ran, unopposed, for the position of Grand Polaris. Edgar (DC Slick) Johnson accepted the office of Grand-Vice Polaris– also unopposed. The remaining appointed officers were:

David Hayden … Grand Executive Secretary
Benjamin Lewis … Grand Treasurer
Lamont Bland … Grand Historian
Charles Brown … Newsletter Editor

Special tribute should be paid to this administration for it marked the beginning of a new lease on life for the fraternity. The new, energetic Grand Polaris scheduled meetings in the northern and southern areas to appeal for cooperation and allegiance. In these encounters, problems and misconceptions were discussed and all back fines and fees were waived. It was imperative to regain confidence in and respect for the national body. The emphasis was placed upon the future while trying to simultaneously instill a sense of fraternity pride. Slowly, through the association of brothers from various chapters, the organization began rebuilding on a stronger basis. To be sure, there were many serious problems: there were a handful of chapters who still had little respect for central authority; and the transition period was hampered by poor or little used communication links.

In any case, the second annual conclave, held in October of 1972, produced an encouraging showing and witnessed the second presentation of the Tony Watson Award. This award for the most outstanding chapter was presented to the Zeta Chapter of North Carolina A & T. the ensuing year was pretty much devoted to reconstruction of the chapters in the Middle-Atlantic region and the creation of interest groups and chapters in the New England area (Boston University and Northeastern University).

The third annual conclave in October 1973 included the presentation of two new individual achievement awards: the most outstanding graduate brother (John House) and the most outstanding undergraduate brother (Clyde Travis). The Tony Watson Award went to Nu Chapter of the University of Maryland. These awards are intended to recognize achievement as well as promote constructive, interfraternity competition. The results have been quite gratifying. Interest in Iota Phi Theta among brothers and non brothers is at an all-time high, four promising graduate chapters have emerged; the renaissance of Alpha Omega in Baltimore; Beta Omega in the Washington, DC area; Gamma Omega in Norfolk, Virginia, and Delta Omega in Boston, Massachusetts.

IOTA PHI THETA -- 1974 through 1976

Calendar year 1974 marked the establishment of regional offices to allow greater communication and easier access to the policy-making apparatus. Regional meetings conducted by the Grand Council were to assist chapters to:

Boost membership

Coordinate pledge policies

Air gripes, problems and differences

A meeting in the Southern region (February 1974) resulted in a revitalized Zeta Chapter, which, subsequently, inducted twenty-seven (27) new brothers. Simultaneously, a meeting at Delaware State was attended by brothers from Gamma, Epsilon, Omicron, Mu and Nu Chapters. Among the issues addressed was the future of Gamma and Epsilon Chapters whose memberships had fallen drastically. A follow-up regional meeting at the Zeta Chapter with brothers from Alpha and Omicron resulted in a revitalized Kappa Chapter at Winston-Salem.

Also during 1974, the following chapters were founded:

Sigma – Boston College

Tau – American International College

Epsilon – Southern Illinois (Carbondale)

Now we were twenty-one (21) chapters strong.

On July 13, 1974, the First Annual Unity Picnic was held in Rock Creek Park, Washington, DC The event was well attended by brothers from all parts of the East Coast.

The year 1975 saw three significant events: Iota's 22nd Undergraduate Chapter was founded at Glassboro State College in New Jersey. Phi Chapter came into existence with twelve (12) new brothers.

Also, on July 4, 1975, Alpha Omega Chapter in Baltimore became the first graduate chapter to induct a pledge line. The first graduate pledge line, called the "Quiet Storm," consisted of five brothers:

James Bright
Russell Gilliam
Harvey Harris
Lyles Purdie, Jr.
Maurice Wood, Jr.

Finally, 1975 saw the first Iota Conclave that was held outside of Baltimore. This was due to a tremendous team effort by the brothers in the New England region to host the 12th Annual Conclave in Boston, Massachusetts.

Calendar year 1976 brought the founding of five new chapters:

Chi – Boston State College
Psi – Coppin State College (Baltimore)
Omega – Western New England College
Alpha Alpha – Stockton College
Alpha Beta – Southern Illinois University (Edwardsville)

On June 19, 1976, the first graduate level conference was held in Baltimore City. Sponsored by Alpha Omega Chapter, the conference provided a forum for existing graduate brothers to discuss their concerns and begin work on organizational problems. In addition, for the first time in a number of years, a serious bid is being made for the office of Grand Polaris. This signifies growth and maturity on the part of the membership and gives us hope for the coming years:

The incumbent national officers as of this writing are:

Thomas Dean ... Polaris.... Five Years Service

Edgar Johnson ... Vice-Polaris... Five Years Service
Joshua Bessicks ... Secretary... Five Years Service
Benjamin Lewis, III ... Treasurer... Five Years Service
Arkley Johnson ... Historian... Three Years Service
Thurman McClain ... Newsletter Editor... Two Years Service

EPILOGUE–

This document serves to pull together the most significant events and traditions of Iota Phi Theta over the first thirteen (13) years. The new Iota Phi Theta is a dynamic entity which is constantly changing and growing. The overwhelming response to the efforts of the Grand Council to unify the fraternity is indicative of the new surge of power and the reconstituted vitality of graduate and undergraduate chapters alike. But this can only be considered the beginning: we must continue to maintain our high standards, reaffirm our commitments and rally to the leadership of the fraternity. In all of this, we must look to our heritage as we mold our future, for truly, "what is past is prologue."

7TH GRAND POLARIS
JOHN HOUSE

"As Iota Phi Theta continues to grow and be impactful, leadership remains critically important. We've been blessed with great leaders at all levels, who have navigated the fraternity to where we are today. Our Grand Polari set the highest standards in moving us forward to greatness. Grand Polari continue to be our guiding light."

IOTA PHI THETA FRATERNITY, INC.
ONE FOCUS. ONE DIRECTION. ONE FRATERNITY.

Photo and articled provided by Brother John House, 15 A'67 Pied Piper

I am John Wesley House Jr. 15A 67. Born in Baltimore at 519 Paca St, South Baltimore. Primary and secondary schooling in the Baltimore School System. 2d of 5 children of John and Evelyn House. Graduated from Edmondson High school in June of '65 and matriculated at Morgan State College in the fall of '65. 1st in my family to attend college. No scholarships. My father suggested that I not go to college but work in a local factory where he was the head caretaker. With my mother's encouragement I decided to go to Morgan. I had visited the campus once and sat in on a class taught by Howard Rawlings who went on to become a prominent political figure in Baltimore and major Morgan State benefactor. The cost of tuition for my first semester was $92.00. It was a struggle to raise that much money, but my mother and uncle came through. My first 2 years at Morgan State I had to take the bus to school from West Baltimore -a 2 hour ordeal both ways . Finally got a '55 Chevy Belair that I used to take other students to school for their bus fares. Their fares paid for my gas and lunch.

I had been approached by a member of Phi Beta Sigma as a potential pledge candidate by a member of the Ira Aldridge Players -Morgan State

College s drama club. Unfortunately, my GPA at that time was not a 2.5 which was the minimum required to pledge for a Greek Fraternity. My 1st year at Morgan was a struggle. I was placed on Academic probation after the 1st year but had gotten my GPA up to 2.3 after attending summer school, which was sufficient at that time to pledge Iota. I knew little about the fraternity other than knowing a few members of the most recent pledge line-THE TRIFLING 28. One evening as I was crossing the campus, my best friend at the time said he was going to the Iota smoker, and I might want to go. I had no idea what a smoker was but went anyway. The smoker, now referred to as an intake session, went very well. The brothers all had on their brown and gold sweaters and as each member was introduced, they did the Iota handshake with the Polaris at that time who was Robert Half Young. These guys were the best looking, best dressed men on campus. They dated the best-looking women and they had cars. I decided I wanted to get in with this group and be one of them. The fraternity was composed of mostly local Baltimore brothers and was a new fraternity with only one chapter, Alpha chapter.

Through a campaign of misinformation led mostly by Founder Lonnie Spruill we were convinced Iota Phi Theta was a national fraternity with numerous chapters replete with regional and national conclaves. They even had a chalet in Arizona available to all financial brothers. A few weeks later I was on the Iota pledge line with about 23 other aspiring Centaurs.

Several of the Iotas on campus were from my high school, Edmondson High, or were from West Baltimore. I was familiar with them, but not close. Some were athletes or otherwise popular personalities. Everybody knew them and I felt getting into this group would certainly help my fledgling social life.

My best friend was Jesse Black. We had gone to the same high school and he knew most of the Trifling 28, specifically, Gary Burgess, Track and football star, Howard Stanbach, football star Raymond Allmond, and wrestler Mac Mclellan. They were locals and after pledging they became life-long friends.

The pledge period was for six weeks and started the first week of March. Of the 20 who survived the six weeks fifteen were from outside of Baltimore. I knew none of them. They were all good guys and we bonded quickly. Eddie Hayes from Jacksonville Florida was elected Line President. My line number was 15 as we went from shortest to tallest. I had a part time job while pledging as a janitor at a local Catholic High school which saved me from some of the punishment the other Centaurs endured. We became Centaurs after the first 2 weeks of pledging. Because I was not well known or even recognized visually by some of the big brothers early on I was able to avoid some physical abuse. Some nights I stayed on campus sleeping on the floor in Eddie Hayes room. One night a knock came on the door around 11:00 p.m. I was on the floor. Hayes opened the door and it was a group of big brothers led by Sluggy Jackson (Reggie Jackson s brother). They grabbed Hayes and took him for a special session. They didn't recognize me and left me by mistake . I believe they made him drink cheap wine in addition to physical activity. He came back around 300am and was definitely not ready for classes that day.

The pledge experience got rough at times and often included being "stroked " with wooden paddles and straw brooms. The tougher it got the more we pulled together and relied on each other to get us all through. We had some talented young men on our line, especially songwriters, singers, and dancers. We performed on campus in one form or another about once a week. Our performances were so good young ladies from the dormitories would come out even after curfew to watch us. Thus we adopted the name the Pied Pipers as our line name which was the idea of brother Bernard Hamm. Our main lead singers were Thomas Dean of Dallas Texas and George Nock of Philadelphia. Our lyricists included Earl Holmes, Robert Hawkins, and Adam Jones. Our choreographers were Ruffin Bell and Ivan Harlee. The songs we developed in 68/69 are still being sung throughout the fraternity today.

At that time Iota Phi Theta was a Greek letter fraternity in name only. We were not members of the Pan Hellenic Council but a member of the Council of Independent Organizations(CIO). We were not considered major players on Morgan's campus, so we wanted to change that once we went over. Each line brother contributed to that goal in some way.

Our Dean of Pledgees was Ronald Jones of the Trifling 28. He was the right Dean for our line and we owe him a debt of gratitude for helping to mold us into the force we became. May he rest in peace.

We crossed the burning sands on April 20th 1967 with a lot of fanfare and celebrating. As we pledged, we did not get to interact with many of the founders as they had mostly graduated or otherwise moved on. The one Founder we interacted with the most was Charles Briscoe. He would hide us from the Big Brothers when we pledged, and we could count on him to make certain beverage purchases for us and consume them with us. He was 100 percent for us and was always available. Through his efforts we scored our first campus wide victory. He designed a float that took 1st Place in the Homecoming parade in the fall of 1968. That was the beginning of wonderful things to come.

When we came into the fraternity our history was handed to us in a spiral notebook which was lost the following year. We had little to no money in the treasury and no clear plan for the future. We did have bylaws and a grand council policy on paper with no bodies in place. We only had two years to make an impact before we graduated. So we went right to work. Robert Hawkins and Earl Holmes had contacts at Hampton Institute and Delaware State College. We initiated those two chapters in the fall of '68 though we had no formal policy and procedures guide in place. Ruffin Bell had contacts at Virginia State University which became a new chapter in the spring of '69. We had seven chapters by the summer of 1969. We were rolling. The road trips to make the chapters were fun and exciting. We were often accompanied by members of the Trifling 28. The last chapter we took over is The University of the District of Columbia.

In the summer of 1968 while at ROTC summer camp I met a cadet from The University of Iowa who said he was a Member of Iota

Phi Theta- the I FELT A THIGH fraternity, which was also one of our mottos. Shocked with this news I was able to get our chapter to do a corporate search to verify our corporate status. We were not incorporated and neither was the Iowa group. We hired a law firm which included the brother of Founder Michael Williams to incorporate our fraternity as a Maryland corporation. We had $300 in our treasury and each of us contributed to pay the $700 legal fee. We were officially incorporated October 31, 1968. Signers of the Articles of incorporation were Danny Henson, Wesley Jennings and John House.

Patricia Dunaway and I were married December 9, 1972. We have two children, Gregory and Taleya House. I spent 35 years as a Sales Manager at Pfizer Pharmaceuticals, the first African American to be inducted into the Pfizer Hall of Fame.

I was inactive from the fraternity for about 20 years due to work relocations. Thomas Dean was initiating a new graduate chapter in Baltimore in 2013 and asked me to join.

Against my protestations I became the 1st elected Polaris of Gamma Omicron Omega Graduate chapter and we became the largest graduate chapter in the fraternity.

At a recent Conclave the fraternity initiated a 10-year Strategic Plan. I chaired The Membership Committee, and our Strategic Plan goals are currently on the Fraternity's website.

I am currently the chair of The Council of Former Grand Polaris. Our role is to advise and be a resource for the fraternity's leadership and membership.

56 years later I am honored to be an active and financial member of Iota Phi Theta, Inc

John W. House, Jr

15 A '67

7th Grand Polaris

Photo and article provided by Brother Edgar 'Amos' Johnson

Edgar Amos Johnson was born in Washington DC in the 1940's to Reverend and Mrs. Richard Johnson. He attended public schools until 1964, when his father was appointed as District Superintendent with the Methodist Church. He graduated from Baltimore City College in June 1966 and enrolled at Morgan State College in September.

He majored in Physical Education and initially planned to pledge Omega Psi Phi because his Father and two brothers were

Ques. In addition. he was named after Bishop Edgar Amos Love, one of Omega's Founders; however, he changed his mind and was initiated in Iota Phi Theta Fraternity, Inc. on April 23, 1969 with 20 other Centaurs. During his Senior year, he served as Iota's representative to the Council of Independent Organizations.

Edgar graduated from Morgan in 1970 with a BS degree. He initially taught Health and Physical Education at DC's Taft Junior High School. A year later, he was hired as an Assistant Community Center Director with the Maryland National Capital Park and Planning Commission. The Commission offered him an opportunity to obtain a Master's degree in Recreation Administration and Supervision at either the University of Maryland or Morgan State. He graduated from Morgan in 1975. Along with 5 other Iota's he established Beta Omega Alumni Chapter in 1970 and was selected as Polaris. In 1971, Thomas "Tex" Dean and Edgar were elected as the Grand Polaris the Grand Vice Polaris respectively.

They initially started new undergraduate chapters at Bowie State College, the University of Maryland, Northeastern University and numerous other colleges in the South, New England and the Midwest. In addition, they made several Alumni Chapters up and down the East Coast. They served in those positions until 1976. Edgar was offered a job as an Outdoor Recreation Planner with the Georgia Department of Natural Resources in 1976. White there, he started Alpha Gamma Chapter at Morris Brown College in Atlanta. Edgar, Fred Lee, Ed Wood and Patrick Conners started Epsilon Omega Alumni Chapter in Atlanta. He was recruited by Wallace Green, a fellow Morgan graduate to join the US Department of the Interior in Washington, DC.

Edgar moved to Columbia, Maryland and established the Psi Omega along with other Iotas and was elected as the Polaris. Former Grand Polaris Allan Eason stepped down and Edgar and Jimmy Martin were selected as the Grand Polaris and Grand Vice Polaris. They asked Reggie Williams and Robert Williams to serve as the

Grand Secretary and Grand Treasurer. Edgar served as the Chair of the Board of Directors for several years. Former Grand Polaris Larry Frazier appointed him to the National Iota Foundation. Former Grand Polaris Karl Price appointed Edgar as the Grand Historian during his Administration. He currently serves as the Parliamentarian of Beta Phi Omega Alumni Chapter in Prince George's County, Maryland.

Edgar is married to Cynthia Johnson and has three children, three grandchildren and four great grandchildren. He and his family worship at Reid Temple AME Church in Glendale, Maryland. When they enter Church, there is a beautiful bronze life-sized Sculpture of Christ on the Cross. The Sculpture was designed by late Brother George Nock, a member of the Infamous "Pied Pipers' ' line which crossed at Alpha Chapter on April 20, 1967.

14TH GRAND POLARIS
JAMES MARTIN

"As I reflect on the 54 years of our organization and my 44 years of service to this great fraternity, I am humbled and honored to see the continued growth of this organization and the many accomplishments of the Brotherhood of Iota Phi Theta Fraternity, Inc.

Looking forward to our continued success as we celebrate our 36th International Conclave in Orlando, Florida."

IOTA PHI THETA FRATERNITY, INC.
ONE FOCUS, ONE DIRECTION, ONE FRATERNITY

Photo and article provided by Brother James Martin

In 1973, Iota Phi Theta Fraternity, Inc. chartered the Omicron Chapter at Northeastern University in Boston, Massachusetts. Omicron Chapter was the first charter line of 34 members (Spring 1973) established in the New England Region. Bro. Clyde Travis (Nu Chapter), Former Grand Polari, Tex Dean, and Edgar Johnson were instrumental in the chapter's founding. I was on the first pledge line of 13 (Fall 1973), "Pharaoh's Army," 3 'O' 73. Omicron's founding led to the chartering of Boston College, Boston University, and other chapters in Western Massachusetts and Hartford, Connecticut. Subsequently, Delta Omega Alumni Chapter, located in Boston, was the first Alumni Chapter in New England which later became the Mid-Atlantic I Region. Iota Phi Theta was a diverse group of men majoring in many disciplines, including Engineering, Criminal Justice, Computer Science, Journalism, and Political Science. During those days, we needed to illustrate to local high school students the achievements of Black students at the University level. At that time, we were fortunate to meet Honorable Founder Webster Lewis. Founder Lewis taught at the New England Conservatory of

Music. In 1975, Omicron Chapter hosted Iota's first Conclave in New England, and Founder Lewis conducted a concert, "A Salute to the Black Recording Companies in America." I served in leadership as the Polaris of Omicron Chapter and Delta Omega Alumni Chapter. In 1976, I graduated from Northeastern, moved to Maryland, and joined Beta Omega Alumni Chapter.

Later I was selected to be the Mid-Atlantic I and II Regional Director under Grand Polaris Allen Eason's administration from 1976–1978. In 1978, I ran and was elected Grand Vice-Polaris under Grand Polaris Edgar Johnson's Administration from 1978–82. In 1984, I was elected Grand Polaris, where Bro. Bruce Nesbitt served as Grand Vice Polaris from 1984–1990. The highlights of the administration were the start of the Mini-Conclave meetings. We held these meetings in the off years of the national Conclave. We also created the Board of Directors. At that time, the Board of Directors was an advisory board. We also started the Life Membership program in 1987. We developed the first membership card and certificate program for brothers. We developed a monthly newsletter, a series of stories, and updates on fraternity activities to augment the Centaur Magazine.

We celebrated the 25th Anniversary celebration of Iota Phi Theta Fraternity, Inc. in Baltimore, MD, at the Omni Hotel. As the fraternity expanded, we held a conclave in the Midwest region in Chicago, Ill, and the first Conclave in the Far West, San Francisco & Oakland, CA, in 1989. Currently I am: Member of the Psi Omega Alumni Chapter in Columbia, Maryland. I, along with Former Grand Polaris Edgar Johnson and Former Grand Secretary Raymond Jenkins, founded Psi Omega Alumni Chapter in Columbia, MD, in 1987. Member of the Council of Former Grand Polari, serving as secretary under chairman Bro. John House. I am also a member of the Strategic Plan Committee, serving as the Quality Assurance Committee Chairman. On September 21-24, 2023, Omicron Chapter will be celebrating its 50th Anniversary on the campus of Northeastern University in Boston.

Photo and article provided by Ted Stephens

For the majority of my life, I have been content to listen to the Lord and be guided by His direction. That very same approach is how I found Iota Phi Theta. Whether it was me heeding God's direction or just plain serendipity, my experience with this fraternity has taken the course of most love affairs (starting out with attraction, moving to obsession and becoming something which is an integral part of your life).

I have had the opportunity to charter two chapters in Iota. After chartering Phi Chapter with the 12 "Bad News" brothers at Glassboro State College (now Rowan University), I partnered with another group of men of good will and chartered Phi Omega, the first Alumni Chapter in New Jersey. But, in 1989 I had one of the pivotal conversations of my life with a late great Iota named Michael Gilbert who, like me, was contemplating a run for Grand Council. In short, Mike encouraged me to run for Grand Polaris and declared, if I ran, he would not. I could not have sought a greater endorsement.

From 1990-1995 I had the unparalleled pleasure to serve as the 15th Grand Polaris. It was a labor of love that I shared with what I regard as the most talented Grand council ever assembled and some of my closest friends; ie. Grand Vice Polaris Jerry O. Pittman, Grand Treasurer Shelton ``Speedy" Barron, Grand Recording Secretary Clifton "Chief" Durant, Grand Corresponding Secretary Troy James and Acting Executive Director Duane Dixon; then formed the core of a great team.

The fact that we loved and respected each other is what made that experience so special. Collectively, my administration made several significant accomplishments;

Held first Conclave in the NJ/NY area jointly hosted by N.J. and N.Y. Graduate Chapters.

First recognized regional leaders as "Region Polari," rather than Region Directors (this made our nomenclature consistent).

Held first and only international Conclave in Jamaica. This was a logistical feat in that brothers could leave from numerous points of departure around the country. (It was a blast!)

Filed and received IRS certification of the National Iota Foundation as a 501(C) (3) corporation.

Established the first membership intake procedure. As a result, Iota became the first black Greek organization to abolish pledging.

Transitioned Conclaves from annual to Bi-annual events. This was essential because of the lack of National Staff (Before that change it was difficult for Grand Councils to do more than to plan the following Conclave and annual summer conferences).

Initiated the first earnest attempt to standardize fraternity operations by revising the operations and procedure manual.

Changed the term of the Grand Council from three years to two years. The goal was to make serving more appealing to busy professionals.

Developed a new Grand Council leadership platform where the Grand Vice Polaris supervised the Regional Polari. (This helped Regions function more uniformly. Also, under the direction of the Grand Vice, Regional Polari could develop their leadership skills and prepare for higher aspirations).

Irrespective of anything set forth above, perhaps the most impactful accomplishment was to take Iota Phi Theta out of our comfort zone and actively engage the National Pan Hellenic council (NPHC) – then known as the "Elite Eight." J.PDuane and I traversed the country, often at our own expense, to market Iota Phi Theta as a worthy entrant to NPHC. This often required that I "self-invite" myself to meetings of other national presidents. This effort proved beneficial on two fronts. First, being exposed to the men of Iota Phi Theta (many had never met an Iota) tore down many ill-conceived opinions held by NPHC organizations about this fraternity. Perhaps more importantly, that effort alleviated fears, seemingly held by some Iotas, that the history, experiences, and/or membership of this august body was any less than our older and larger brother and sister organizations.

Our efforts were arduous, but successful. Iota Phi Theta began receiving actual invitations to events hosted by NPHC organizations. In 1993, I became the first Grand Polaris invited to speak at the Phi Beta Sigma national meeting when I attended their national convention in Charlotte, NC in 1993. The rest, as they say, is history. After that it was a "fait accompli" – Iota Phi Theta would win significant friends (like the late DST Daisy Wood) and influence other people to eventually gain induction into the NPHC, in 1996.

This would forever convert the erstwhile Elite Eight into the Divine Nine of today.

Photo taken by Brother Al Michael
Brothers Wayne Dorseyn, Jerry Pittman, unknown Brother and Ted Stephens
Iotas in Ocho Rios, Jamaica
First International Conclave
Circa 1993

Photo taken by Brother Al Michael
Grand Polaris Ted Stephens, Jerry Pittman and Rondell James

Photo taken by guest of Al Michael
Iotas by the Sea
Iotas and friends and family getting ready to climb Dunns River Fall in unison.

Photo taken by guest of Al Michael
Iotas climbing the Dunns River Fall in unison.

Photo and article provided by Brother Jerry Pittman

JERRY 'JP' PITTMAN
16TH INTERNATIONAL GRAND POLARIS

"The steps of a good man are ordered by the Lord: and He delighted in his way."
Psalm 37:23

On April 12, 1973, my steps were ordered by God to become a Brother of Iota Phi Theta Fraternity, Inc. And this year, 2023, I will celebrate 50 years of brotherhood. I am proud to say during these 50 years, I have remained both financially and active in the organization that I love.

On the campus of then Morgan State College, and now Morgan State University, I pledged with 13 Dynamic Brothers who were known as the 'Black Militant Railroad.' IOTA has never been the same.

My fraternal history is as follows: I have served as Chapter Polaris, Regional Polaris, and the Director of both Undergraduate and Graduate Affairs. I also was the recipient of the James Anthony Watson Undergraduate and Graduate Brother of the Year Awards.

I assisted my deceased son, my legacy, Evan Jerron Pittman in establishing the Theta Sigma Chapter of Iota on the campus of Sacred Heart University, a predominantly white institution. We are still the first and only African American Greek organization on the Sacred Heart University campus in 2023.

I also was the first Grand Polaris to represent the Fraternity in Ebony Magazine.

From 1990 to 1995, I had the distinct pleasure of serving as the International Grand Vice Polaris under our 16th International Grand

Polaris, Theodore N. Stephens, II and what a team we had. I was given the task of managing our Regional Polari. What a rewarding experience it was for me to groom fellow brothers in leadership development.

A huge thank you to my Brothers, Rondall 'RJ' James, Steve Birdine, Richard Gilbert, Robert Clark, Karl Price, Dennis Allen and the late Aubrey Smith.

What a talented group of young men! Three of those gentlemen later became IGP's and one became a Grand Vice Polaris.

Ted and I worked on several projects which carried over to my administration and together we were able to expand the fraternity's territory and broaden the horizons of the organization.

A huge thank you, to our 15th IGP, Theodore Stephens, II, for allowing me to stand on his shoulders which not only equipped but also prepared me to become the 16th International Grand Polaris.

From 1995 to 1999, I was honored to serve as your 16th International Grand Polaris. My close friend and Brother, Rondall 'RJ' James joined my team as my Grand Vice Polaris. My Grand Secretaries were the late Clifton 'Chief' Durant and Robert Clark. My Grand Treasurers were Shelton 'Speedy' Barron and Ben 'Granddad' Lewis. A HUGE 'Thank you' to Dwayne 'Romeo' Dixon who served as my Executive Director. As a volunteer, Dwayne went the second mile for the fraternity. Thank you to all who served. It was extremely busy with the day to day operation of the fraternity, i.e., publishing newsletters, chartering and reactivating chapters, conducting Grand Council meetings and attending Regional meetings. My administration did it all and they enjoyed doing it.

We had several goals, and I am proud to say we achieved them all:
- Having Eta Chapter on the campus of Virginia State University reinstated after a five-year suspension.
- Engaging both, our Eternal Sweetheart Audrey Brooks and our Founders in a way they have never been involved before.

Our Eternal Sweetheart attended two conclaves, a national picnic and several other fraternity events.

In fact, I will never forget when we were in Oakland, California and she took the stage to give her remarks. Eternal Sweetheart Audrey Brooks said, "I feel like Halle Berry."

- I had the pleasure of interviewing 11 of 12 Founders and I talked to them about the Fraternity in 1963 versus 1995. They could not believe how much we had grown and developed over the years. I expressed to them the significance of having their involvement and the blessing of having Founders who are still alive. As a result of our interview, eight of the Founders became active.

- Ted, Dwayne and I laid the foundation for Iota Phi Theta to become a member of the National Pan-Hellenic Council. We met and garnered the support of the late Daisy Wood of Delta Sigma Theta Sorority, Inc. I made some trips with Brother Ted as we aimed to showcase and market our great fraternity. Becoming a member of the NPHC became a priority because our Undergraduate Chapters were not being recognized on their college and university campuses as a Greek organization. Brother Ted passed me the microphone, Dwayne lived on the computer and Daisy Wood continued to mentor us. The grand finale was having seven IOTA Founders attend our NPHC Induction Ceremony in February 1997. The Elite 8 is officially the Divine 9!

- Under my administration we purchased the fraternity's first National Headquarters, known as 'Founders Hall.' This was a huge undertaking and all I can say is, "To God be the Glory."

A special thanks to our 15th IGP Ted Stephens, 17th IGP Rondall James, Ben Lewis, Dan Henson, and certainly our Real Estate Genius, Carolyn Syphax-Young.

- Under our administration, we were able to raise the chapter and national dues for the first time in a number of years.

Finally, we wanted to leave the Fraternity with some money and we did. I would be remiss if I didn't give a shout-out to my soulmate and lovely wife of thirty-five years, Mrs. Adrienne Walker-Pittman. Adrienne had a severe tragedy when I was only one year into my term of office, and she would not allow me to resign. What a wonderful support system.

Thank you for allowing me and having the confidence in me to serve as your 16th International Grand Polaris. But most of all, thank you for your respect and support over the years.

Yours In The Fold,
Jerry 'JP' Pittman

ACKNOWLEDGMENTS

With a special shout-out to:
Brother Harold David Ford (5 A '66)
Sergeant at Arms
Brother Harold "Sonny" Jennifer III (17 A '66) a.k.a. "Lord North"
Brother Dr, Richard B. Speaks (25 A '66) a.k.a. "Senior Suave"
Brother Ronald Fassett (14 A '66) a.k.a. "Dinky"
Brother Robert Redd (12 A '67) a.k.a. "Boston Redds"
Brother Kevin Bennett Executive Director
Brother Anthony Workman a.k.a. "Capp"

APPENDIX
THE LINEAGE OF ALPHA/ALPHA OMEGA

THE 1960'S CHAPTER LINES OF ALPHA CHAPTER

SEPTEMBER 19, 1963
"THE FOUNDERS OF IOTA PHI THETA"
ALBERT HICKS
LONNIE SPRUILL
CHARLES BRISCOE
FRANK COAKLEY
JOHN SLADE
BARRON WILLIS
WEBSTER LEWIS
CHARLES BROWN
LOUIS HUDNELL
CHARLES GREGORY
ELIAS DORSEY JR.
MICHAEL WILLIAMS

1964 "THE 15 CENTAURS"
1A64 RICHARD V. JOHNSON
2A64 FREDERICK HOWARD
3A64 RONALD FLAMER
4A64 WESLEY JENNINQS
5A64 JEFF JOHNSON
6A64 DANIEL HENSON

7A64 WILLIE BARBER

8A64 HAROLD ADAMS

9A64 RONALD WHEATLEY

10A64 JEROME CULLENS

11A64 LAWRENCE BROOKS

12A64 JAMES A. WATSON

13A64 HOWARD WILLIAMS

14A64 CALVIN FREELAND

15A64 CHARLES WATTS

1965 "THE ONE AND ONLY"

1A65 AL PIERCE

1966 "TRIFLING 28"

1A66 ROBERT YOUNG, PRESIDENT

2A66 NORMAN E. JOHNSON, JR. VICE PRESIDENT

3A66 EDWARD ALLEN EASON, III SECRETARY

4A66 DWIGHT STITH, TREASURER

5A66 HAROLD D. FORD, SERGEANT-AT-ARMS

6A66 RAYMOND B. ALLMOND

7A66 PHILLIP B. BAPTISTE

8A66 GARY L. BURGESS

9A66 JOSEPH CHAPLAN

10A66 EDWARD C. COHEN

11A66 KENNETH E. CULLINGS

12A66 HARRY CROXTON

13A66 THELPHS A. EVANS

14A66 RONALD A. FASSET

15A66 HENRY B. FORD, JR.

16A66 JAMES E. "SLUGGY" JACKSON

17A66 HAROLD "SONNY" JENNIFER

18A66 ARKLEY B. "PETE" JOHNSON

19A66 DAVIDSON L. JONES

20A66 RONALD G. JONES

22A66 ALFRED R. MICHAEL

21A66 WELFRED MCLELLAND

23A66 JAMES A. PENN

24A66 LAFAYETTE SINGLETON, JR.

25A66 RICHARD B. SPEAKS

26A66 HOWARD STANBACK

27A66 COURTNEY GRANT VALENTINE

28A66 TIMOTHY L. WELDON

1967 "PIED PIPERS"

1A67 EDWARD HAYES

2A67 JOHN S. LANIER

3A67 LOUIS ROBINSON

4A67 ROBERT HAWKINS

5A67 JESSE J.BLACK

6A67 WALTER MITCHELL

7A67 ADAM JONES

8A67 FRED HUNTER

9A67 GEORGE NOCK

10A67 JOSHUA H. BESSICKS, JR.

11A67 THOMAS "TEX" DEAN

12A67 IVAN HARLEE

13A67 CHARLES F. BROWN

14A67 ROBERT REDD

15A67 JOHN HOUSE

16A67 RUFFIN BELL

17A67 ISSAC JACKSON

18A67 BERNARD HAMM

19A67 EARL HOLMES

20A67 EARL WAKE

1968 "PING PONGS"
1A68 ISSAC FLOYD
2A68 ANTHONY EVANS
3A68 MICKEY BARBEE
4A68 ERNEST BARRETT
5A68 ROBERT HARVEY
6A68 JAMES SMITH
7A68 MORTON WALLER
8A68 TOMMY SMITH
9A68 KIRSON HERBERT
10A68 BEN LEWIS
11A68 LUTHER RHONE
12A68 CHICO LYONS
13A68 WILLIAM "LEIGH" SMITH
14A68 HENRY MOUZON
15A68 ALBERT MILLER
16A68 EDDIE PATTERSON
17A68 WILLIAM HARRIS
18A68 GONZALEZ JACOBS
19A68 CALVIN JOHNSON
20A68 WILLIAM MATTHEWS
21A68 NAPOLEON BILES
22A68 DAVID MARSH
23A68 GEORGE FELTON

1969 "FLYING NUNS/FINE LINE OF 69"
1A69 LASALLE REYNOLDS
2A69 KENNETH SMITH
3A69 LEROY AIKEN
4A69 MELVIN WILLIAMS
5A69 LESTER BINNS
6A69 JOHN JONES
7A69 JAMES FISH

8A69 CURTIS WALTKINS
9A69 JOHN SYKES
10A69 ARTHUR JORDAN
11A69 EDWARD MADDEN
12A69 ERNIE HADRICKS
13A69 JULIAN DIXON
14A69 CLIFTON DURANT
15A69 WAYNE JACKSON
16A69 EDGAR JOHNSON
17A69 LAMONT BLAND
18A69 COLLIN NOLE
19A69 FRANK WATSON
20A69 LARRY WATSON
21A69 DARRYL WILSON

1970'S CHAPTER LINES OF ALPHA CHAPTER

1970 "THE PHANTOM TEN"
1A70 WAYNE MITCHELL
2A70 LARRY HARLEE
3A70 CLARENCE HICKS
4A70 RICHARD MATHEWS
5A70 WINSTON HASKINS
6A70 LARRY MARTIN
7A70 CHRISTOPHER YANCEY
8A70 LAVERN RODGERS
9A70 GARY MARTIN
10A70 LESTER BINNS

1971 "OUR GANG"
1A71 ALONZO CHAVIS
2A71 GREGORY DAUGHERTY
3A71 ARTHUR LAWSON

4A71 MILTON MACK
5A71 WAYNE J. DORSEY, JR.
6A71 MELVIN GRAY
7A71 CHARLES WILLIAMS
8A71 JAMES DAVIS
9A71 LARRY MARTIN
10A71 LARRY WARD
11A71 MONTY MARSH
12A71 IRVIN T. DURANT
13A71 ANTHONY FLOYD

1972 "MAGNIFICENT SEVEN"
1A72
2A72
3A72
4A72
5A72
6A72
7A72

1973 "BLACK MILITANT RAILROAD"
1A73 MITCHELL DAVIDSON
2A73 JOHN MARSH
3A73 RICHARD FIELDS
4A73 ISAAC HAYES
5A73 TONY DAVIS
6A73 ERIC TAYLOR
7A73 DWAYNE DIGGS
8A73 RALPH JEFFERSON
9A73 MICHAEL COLLIER
10A73 JERRY "JP" PITTMAN
11A73 PERCY ROGERS
12A73 OTIS JAYE

13A73 KEITH COLLINS
14A73 MARION DEVOE

1974 "HOLLYWOOD SWINGERS"
1A74 ARTHUR ROCHE
2A74 BUZZY
3A74 GARY HINTON
4A74 JOE REED
5A74 BRADY WILLIS
6A74 WARREN MAJOR
7A74 CLAYTON OSBORNE
8A74 REGGIE WILLIAMS
9A74 RICHARD JONES
10A74 JOE SHELTON
11A74 DALE ROBINSON
13A74 WILLIAMS SMITH
14A74 ROBERT WILLIAMS, SR
15A74 CHARLES KIAH
16A74 JOHN EVANS
17A74 LARRY JOYNER
18A74 GERARD POWELL
19A74 ABE
20A74 REGGIE 'POUND CAKE'
21A74
22A74
23A74 ANGELO WELLS
24A74 TIM BAYLOR

1975 "BLACK SURVIVAL 18"
1A75 LEM KENLEY
2A75 MIKE BROWN
3A75 ROBERT WAKE
4A75 DAVID PORTER

5A75 CHARLES KELLY

6A75 ANDRE WELLS

7A75 TONY CREWS

8A75 CLIFF BROWN

9A75 CHARLES CARTER

10A75 JAMES MOBLEY

11A75 KEVIN SLADE

12A75 REGINALD PETROY

13A75 RON NEWMAN

14A75 GERALD HAWKINS

15A75 RAYMOND MERRITT

16A75 RICHARD MCCOY

17A75 VERNON DUNN

18A75 STEVE TURPIN

1976 "NINE DESCENDANTS OF LOVE"

1A76 ROBERT CRAWLEY

2A76 FRED ESANASON

3A76 ROBIN CAPERS

4A76 RONALD CURRY

5A76 KEVIN WILSON

6A76 MICHAEL RAMSEY

7A76 OLANDO SCOTT

8A76 TOMY LOMAX

9A76 BRIAN "DOC" MURRAY

1977 "GANGSTER AVALANCHE"

1A77 THELBERT "T-BIRD" WILLIAMS

2A77 EDDIE WRIGHT

3A77 PAUL HOBSON

4A77 CRAIG WEEKS

5A77 WILLIE CREWS

6A77 VINCE MOORE

7A77 VINCE CAIN

8A77 MIKE DUBOISE

9A77 KEITH BLACKMON

10A77 SYLVESTER VAUGHN

11A77 ERNIE BELL

12A77 MAURICE BROOKS

13A77 DREXLER CARTER

14A77 MAURICE BURTON

15A77 JAN SLEETS

16A77 BUTCH THOMAS

17A77 BILLY KING

18A77 MIKE MORGAN

19A77 GREGG YELDELL

20A77 LIONEL DUNCAN

21A77 ROBERT SCOTT

22A77 RON WILLIAMS

23A77 GARFIELD MCCOY

24A77 JOE FOLKES

25A77 GREGORY GIST

26A77 ANDRE WICKHAM

27A77 WILLIAM ASKEW

28A77 MARVIN HICKS

1978 "NEW TESTAMENTS"

1A78 RONALD SHACKLEFORD

2A78 MAURICE CLARK

3A78 DAVE HUTCHINGSON

4A78 KEVIN COLEMAN

5A78 JERRY WEAVER

6A78 MICHAEL BLAND

7A78 KENNY BROWN

8A78 KIETH BUTLER

9A78 DEAC O'MALLY

10A78 STEVE CAMBELL

11A78 ARTHUR COOK

1979 "THE 16TH GENERATION"

1A79 KIETH SERMAN

2A79 RODNEY CARPENTER

3A79 KEVIN WALLACE

4A79 PHILLIP WOMBLE

5A79 CARL BARKLEY

6A79 ROBERT MADISON

7A79 SETH CHISOLM

8A79 CURRY STONE

9A79 TERRY GILBERT

10A79 DAVID McNIEL

THE 1980'S CHAPTER LINES OF ALPHA CHAPTER

1980 SUMMER "THE LONE SURVIVOR"

1A80SU FRANK JONES

"1980 "8 FOR THE 80'S" MINUS 1

1A80 CRAIG SPENCER

2A80 VINCENT WHITE

3A80 CLARENCE HOLZENDOLF

4A80 TROY BROOKS

5A80 MICHAEL "MIKE P" PAYLOR

6A80 HECTOR RISER

7A80 DARREN JENKINS

1981 "DIRTY DOZENS"

1A81 EARNEST "BAMA" DAVIS

2A81 DAVON ISOM

3A81 OTIS LENNON AKA LANCE ROMANCE

4A81 BENTON BARKLEY

5A81 CRAIG BATTLES

6A81 SAM ANDERSON

7A81 BRUCE BROWN

8A81 MASTAR KAMEL

9A81 AL HILL

10A81 THOMAS BEVERLY

11A81 DARRYL BROWN

12A81 GLENN HAZEL

1982 SUMMER "THE SOUL SURVIVOR"

1A82SU JOE WATSON

1982 "11 ON 11 OVER/THE CHRONICLES"

1A82 DARRELL "D.B." BROWN

2A82 RAYNARD "LUCKY LOU" SWEETNEY

3A82 MARK THOMAS

4A82 RAY FISHER

5A82 ESSET TATE, JR

6A82 ROBERT JORDON

7A82 ANTHONY FLOYD

8A82 MICHAEL BROWN

9A82 MARK PATTEN, SR.

10A82 LEON COATES

11A82 BRIAN TYSON

1983 "UNDERGROUND EXPRESS"

1A83 KEITH "KEITH J" JACKSON

2A83 PHIL COLEMAN

3A83 TRACY "BOSTON BEAST" LITTHCOUT

4A83 DERRICK HILL

5A83 RODNEY GRAY

6A83 PAUL HOOD

1984 FALL UNPREDICTABLE NINE/GO-GOS"
1A84 DANNY WATKINS
2A84 GLENN "G LOVE" GIBSON
3A84 SAM BOONE
4A84 CHARLIE COOK, JR.
5A84 ANDREW WOODS
6A84 JOHN "MANIAC" McQUEEN
7A84 ROBERT "MURF" MURPHY
8A84 LADONNE ADAIR
9A84 MIKE GARDNER
1985 "SCHOOLBOYS"
1A85 TED RODGERS, JR.
2A85 JOY M. "JOYSTICK" MOORE
3A85 ALPHONZO FLUTE
4A85 JEFF "KID SMOOTH" GIBSON
5A85 ERIC "E-ROCK" SMITH
6A85 DREW "DC" CARR
7A85 COY "CDB" BURKE
8A85 TONY "TEE" SCOTT
9A85 SEMP TAYLOR

1986 "NEW ATTITUDE"
1A86 TYRONE ROGERS
2A86 EDDIE JACKSON
3A86 NEAL RICHARDS
4A86 JOHN CARY
5A86 JAMES SCHULER
6A86 LEE "TUBBS" JERKINS
7A86 RICHARD MCCLAIN
8A86 FREDRICK MONTGOMERY
9A86 JEFFREY RUFFIN
10A86 ERIC HINES
11A86 CLIFF DAVIS

12A86 CHAUNCEY WYNN
13A86 JOHN CURTIS
14A86 TYRONE PERTEE
15A86 MAURICE WATKINS

1987 "THE CHOSEN FEW"
1A87 MARIO BARR
2A87 GILBERT KING
3A87 NORMAN "YURI" FORBES
4A87 AL DAIS
5A87 PAUL PENDERGRASS
6A87 NOEL LIVERPOOL

1988 SPRING "THE UNTOUCHABLES"
1A88SP JAMES DOZIER
2A88SP KEITH SINGLETON
3A88SP DARRY GREER
4A88SP RAYLON ADAMS

1988 SUMMER "THE ODD COUPLE MINUS ONE"
1A88SU NATHAN AYERS

1988 FALL "THE DISORDERLIES"
1A88FA CRISPUS HEDGEMANN
2A88FA WAYNE JACKSON
3A88FA CHARLES "CHUCK" PEARSON
4A88FA MARCUS "SONNY" SMITH

THE 1990'S CHAPTER LINES OF ALPHA CHAPTER

1990 SPRING "LET'S DO IT AGAIN"
1A90SP DONTAE SMITH
2A90SP DEQUAN DINKINS

3A90SP COREY WILLIAMS
4A90SP MARK LAWRENCE
5A90SP FELIX CHANEY
6A90SP LES HATCHER
7A90SP DARIN ALLEN
8A90SP VERNARDO "BOND" MCNEIL
9A90SP KEVIN O'CONNOR

1991 SUMMER "LAID BACK JUST CHILLIN"
1A91SU CLINTON COLE

1991 SPRING "SEVEN DAY PROCESS"
1A91SP MICHEAL JACKSON

1991 SPRING "_____"
1A91SP BRIAN JONES
2A91SP DIAMOND BLOUNT
3A91SP HORRACE MINYFIELD
4A91SP JAMAL RAMOS

1993 SPRING "ONCE AGAIN IT'S ON"
1A93SP LOEL REINHART
2A93SP CHARLTON WOODY
3A93SP CEDRIC THOMAS
4A93SP KEVIN SMITH
1993 FALL "FLAT LINE"
1A93FA DARRIOUS HILL
2A93FA JESSIE JONES

1994 SPRING "DYNAMIC DUO"
1A94SP JEFF NELSON
2A94SP LARRY OWENS

1995 FALL "FIRST DEGREE, SECOND NATURE"
1A95FA GERARD DESIR

1995 SPRING "THE LOST TRIBE"
1A95SP ERIC MCCOY
2A95SP AHMAD ALI
3A95SP OMAR MARTIN

1996 FALL "THE ONLY ONE LEFT STANDING"
1A96FA SHERMAN BRAXTON

1997 SUMMER "NEW HORIZONS"
1A97SU WILLIAM CAFFEE

1997 FALL "NO WAY OUT"
1A97FA SHAWN MORRIS
2A97FA AYANDA ADEBOWALE ONI II

1998 SUMMER "GHETTO FABULOUS"
1A98SU MALCOLM LIVERPOOL

1998 FALL "3 TIMES AS TOUGH"
1A98FA RICHARD SMITH
2A98FA FIAD ALI
3A98FA JOHN DOZIER

1999 SPRING "THE RENAISSANCE SIX"
1A99SP DANNY PATTON
2A99SP GRANT COLEMAN
3A99SP JOEY ANDERSON
4A99SP RYAN HARRISON
5A99SP EDDIE ORE
6A99SP OMAR STOKES

1999 SUMMER "ALL ALONE"
1A99FA* TIMOTHY WILLIAMS

1999 FALL "WE LEARN THE HARD WAY"
1A99FA HOWARD PERKINS
2A99FA DESMOND STEWART

THE 2000'S CHAPTER LINES OF ALPHA CHAPTER

2000 SPRING "I2K"
1A00SP EARL MOORMAN
2A00SP ALBERT "A.J" GONZALEZ
3A00SP EDGAR "EDDIE" EVANS
2001 SPRING "DA STRUGGLE"
1A01SP KIETH MCCRY
2A01SP SHERWIN HALL
3A01SP JAMES HILL
2001 FALL "NEW ERA"
1A01FA REGGIE JOHNSON
2A01FA MAJOR MASSENBURG

2002 SPRING "THINGS FALL APART"
1A02SP TERRY MCNAIR
2A02SP JASON ROBERTS
3A02SP TERRY MCCLULLEN

2003 SPRING "THE GOOD, THE BAD, & THE UGLY"
1A03SP DEON HENRY JR.
2A03SP STEVENSON MONCHERY
3A03SP DAMEON PRESCOTT
4A03SP SILAS BERRY
5A03SP TAVONE STEWART
6A03SP LEONARD DIXON

7A03SP JASON ECKLES
8A03SP MARVIN COUNCIL
9A03SP DANIEL ROBINSON JR
2017 FALL "B.M.F. TEFLON DONS"
1AFA17 EVAN "CONTROLLED CHAOS" ROBERTSON
2AFA17 EDWARD YOUNG-MUHAMMAD
3AFA17 JAMES K. GREEN
4AFA17 BRANDON "KAMIKAZE" NSAMELUH
5AFA17 SEAN "NOTORIOUS" ANDERSON, JR.
6AFA17 RODNEY "JARHEAD" HOLMAN
7 AFA17 JOSHUA SMITH
8AFA17 SAHEED "UNBR8KABLE" AKINSOWON
9AFA17 DARYL "MANSLAUGHTER" CONLEY
10AFA17 KASUN THOMPSON
11AFA17 RODNEY "DA TRUTH" MENSAH
TO BE UPDATED IN THE 2 EDITION
Provided by Marcus 'Sonny" Smith, Polaris, Alpha Omega
"Building A Tradition, Not Resting Upon One"

INDEX

www.ingramcontent.com/pod-product-compliance
Lightning Source LLC
LaVergne TN
LVHW050841221224
799689LV00020B/135/J